The Heavenly Trial

A Play in Four Acts

by

Dauvid

authorHOUSE®

AuthorHouse™
1663 Liberty Drive
Bloomington, IN 47403
www.authorhouse.com
Phone: 833-262-8899

Published by AuthorHouse 09/14/2021

ISBN: 978-1-4184-1870-0 (sc)

Print information available on the last page.

Acknowledgments

I wish to thank Mrs. Peggy Mendelson, the President of the Stanford University Bookstores, Inc. for her invaluable advice and editing of the manuscript.

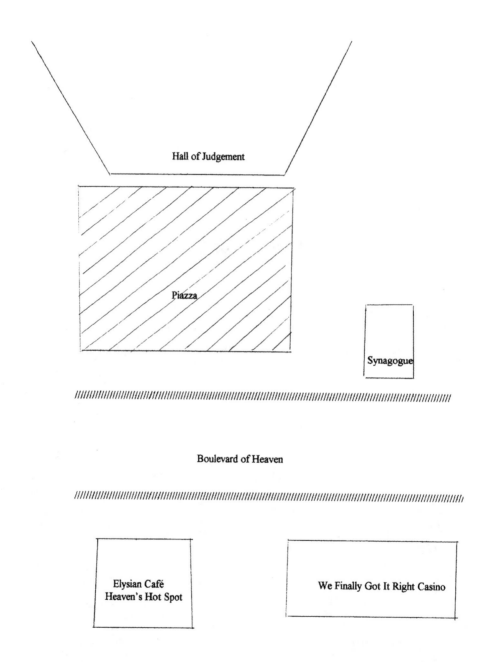

The cast

in the order of their appearance

Metatron	Cerub appointed by God to oversee the visible Universe
Gabriel	Cerub sent to Earth by Metatron
Mr. Snake	Direct from the Garden of Eden
Charley McCarthy	Himself-Edgar Bergan's wooden buddy
Waitress	A soul admitted to Heaven
Cherub 1	
Cherub 2	
Eve	Direct from the Garden of Eden in white robes
Biblical Matriarchs	
Sarah	Dressed in light blue
Rebecca	Dressed in light tan
Rachel	Dressed in pink
Zipporah	Moses' wife, Dressed in purple
Biblical Patriarchs	
Abraham	Dressed in white robes
Jacob	Dressed in shepherd's skirt
Moses	Wooden staff in hand
Noah	Robe with head covered
Soul 1	
Soul 2	
Professor Montaigne	Behavioral Anthropologist
Sigmond Freud	Father of Psychoanalysis
Abigail Adams	Wife of John Adams, American Revolution
Albert Einstein	Father of modern Physics
King of Moab	Biblical King
Niccolo Machiavelli	Author of "The Prince"
Mohammad	
Sol of Tarsus	The Apostle Paul

Glossary

Torah	**The first books of the Bible**
Kabbalah	**Book of Jewish mysticism**
Tehillim	**Book of Psalms**
Kaddish	**Mourner's Prayer**
Oy Veh!	**Woe is me!**
Unga Blysim	**Blow off (almost)**

Contents

Act One

In small theaters, the chorus and dancing may be displayed on video screens to reduce the size of the cast.

Act 1 Scene 1

Off stage the Angel Chorus is singing "Imagination". Between each paragraph of the Moderator's opening, the refrains are accentuated.

Moderator: Our play opens in Heaven. Our Heaven is how man might imagine Heaven to be. *(Angel Chorus) "Imagination"*

While in the Garden of Eden, Adam and Eve led an angelic "happy go lucky" life with their only admonition: "Do no eat from the Tree of Knowledge". Having committed this sin, they no longer resembled angels. They were now Human able to recognize either happiness or sadness. Along with a burgeoning boundless imagination, Men, forever after, gained the free will to make decisions. Occasionally, the decisions were good but usually they were bad-very bad.

Ever since Adam and Eve were expelled from the Garden of Eden, Man has always been fascinated by the "Unrevealed" – about the nature of Heaven, Angels, Man's soul, and God. For thousands of years, to prove Man's sincerity, came forth all kinds of "isms" and religions. One or more days each week are devoted to prove the honesty of each man's zeal.

The chorus singing:
  "Why, oh, why do you cloud your mind?"
  "Closing your eyes in ecstasy."
  "It's no crime, just be good and understood"
  "Without the sake of Fantasy."

Moderator: Heaven is perfectly white with clouds of every pastel shade floating among the Seraphim, the Cherubim, and those Souls who were privileged to be admitted to Heaven. The Seraphim have three pairs of Golden Wings. The Seraphim are the Angels who rested on the top of the Ark that the Israelites carried around the Sinai desert for forty years. The Cherubim are the Angels with white wings guarding the "Gate of Heaven".

The Soul is a rather complicated matter. Any concept of the Soul by man is so complicated that all we can say is that the Soul separates the living from the non-living. Thus the Soul implies that if you were judged by Heaven to have led an exemplary life, your Soul with its corporal adornment might be admitted to Heaven.

The Kabbalah tells us that Metatron, a Cherub, was appointed by God to govern the visible Universe. Metatron has larger white wings to distinguish him from the other Cherubim.

Our scene opens with Metatron walking along the Boulevard of Heaven. Metatron is visibly troubled.

In an undertone, but still audible, the Angel chorus is singing a parody of "What's the use of worrying".

Metatron *(talking aloud to himself)*:

Man is the Crown of Creation-the reason that God created the visible Universe. God has placed Man on Earth to be the guardian over all creatures on the land, in the seas, in the air. For Man's survival, God has planted numerous vegetables, many different fruit trees, grasses with grains and filled the skies with many edible birds-every need that Man could ever wish for.

God cleanses the Earth of dead or dying plants and animals without asking men for any help.

But men have been incessantly destructive in his relations with other human beings. In addition, he kills animals without reason, devastates the land, pollutes the seas, and poisons the air. Has

3

Mankind ever done anything right? All of his ambitions come to naught. Why, Why has he failed? God was almost shaking with rage. It's been quite a while since I have known God to be so angry.

God's words have filled me with an admonition that man is falling, falling into an abyss, which he will never be able to extricate himself.

The Angel Chorus
"What is Heaven like,
With the world as its spike,
Holding upright the tent of Faith
Over the minds of Mortal Man."

Oh, foolish man
Accepting any useless Faith
Walking Earth, lost in resignation
By the fantasy of adoration."

Metatron is strolling down the Boulevard of Heaven when he sees Mr. Snake and the Angel Gabriel coming from the opposite direction towards the Elysian Café. Gabriel is also a Cherub but he is adorned only with small white wings. Mr. Snake is dressed in a superbly tailored Rattlesnake jacket.

Gabriel: Hey, Boss, what's the matter? I've never seen you so agitated. It couldn't be that there is trouble in Paradise.

Metatron: God is troubled, very troubled about Man. With all of his efforts to make Man understand, God has tried endlessly to enlighten men to live in peace with his neighbors, to care for the widow and the needy. Man has been given dominion over all the animals and plants. Man should appreciate his obligations in caring for the land and the waters and the skies. Everything has fallen on closed minds and deaf ears. Mankind is just deaf, dumb, and blind.

Mr. Snake: Why should God be troubled? Man hasn't changed since he and his wife and kids were kicked out of the Garden of Eden. As simple as it is, even the admonition against Murder and Hatred in the story of Cain and Abel is misunderstood. They still think that they can kill any animal just to make a sport of hunting, and they can hate for any reason. Let's relax and go into the Elysian and have a drink. Then we can take our time and discuss the situation.

Gabriel: Now that's a great idea. It's time we relaxed a bit after judging who will be admitted to Heaven and who will have to go the other way. We only let three into heaven today. There were tens of thousands we sent the other way.

Metatron: Even the Cherubim's job at the Gates of Heaven must be getting tougher and tougher. Since men have always known they are mortal, you would think they would give up wondering about Heaven and Immortality.

Mr. Snake: Wondering about Heaven must give them a headache. What do you think, Gabriel?

Metatron: It's got to be more than a headache.

Gabriel: I don't know where they come from but those nutty mystics on Earth think there are spheres or orbits between Heaven and Earth. Then there are palm readers, Tarot card readers who think they predict the future, glass balls used by mystics for séances and druggies-all kinds of screwballs.

It may not be understandable but the more scholarly men become, the more their imaginations wander. They think they can solve any question that comes into their minds. There is one group who call themselves Scientists. Some of them have declared that there is more than one Universe. Another group keeps measuring the distance of the outer limits of the Universe or the age of the Universe . Every couple of years they keep changing that distance or the age of the Universe and this makes them very proud. One guy thinks that Creation began shortly before a tiny bit of matter the size of Mustard seed exploded. As far as I can tell almost all the scientists believe this. None of the scientists have ever questioned where the mustard seed came from. To top all of this, they won't even discuss their opinions with scholars who are not scientists.

Metatron: Gab, man's boundless imaginations is only one of the innumerable other problems on Earth. If they are doing all this wondering, one would think that they would wonder about the purpose of the Universe. All those scholars who are convinced that Man can understand everything, and those so called agnostics who don't know what to believe, the Universe couldn't just happen. With all that God has done for them, they always find some way or reason to screw everything up. What a bunch! What the Hell, let's go in and really hang one on.

Barrelhouse music is easily heard as they approach the café.

The doorman, who is the spitting image of Charley McCarthy and dressed to the hilt in a spotless white uniform with gold epaulettes, gold buttons and gold braid on his sleeves, bows as he opens the door. A Downey woodpecker keeps trying to peck at his head, which gives Charley an opportunity to take a swat at Mr. Snake. He just misses as Mr. Snake ducks away.

Doorman: "Welcome to the Elysian Café, a bit of Earth in Heaven. Our waitresses are gorgeous with curves that won't stop. Our drinks are half priced until 4 o'clock. There's an empty table in the back, but you have only an hour to hang one on at this price.

Act 1 Scene 2

Inside the Elysian Café, Barrelhouse Music with one Cherub at one piano and one Seraphin at a second piano playing "You done me wrong". Scantily dressed waitresses are serving the customers or standing close to the entrance near the bar.

Metatron, Gabriel and Mr. Snake enter the café and are greeted by one of the waitresses. Just as she turns to seat them, Mr. Snake's rattlesnake tattooed arm extends out of his jacket, completely wraps around her waist like a boa constrictor, and pats her on her behind. The waitress turns and smiles adeptly moving away from Mr. Snake.

Mr. Snake: Things are really looking up around here. For an afternoon, this place is really swinging. If the Elysian were on Earth, they could really make a killing. Say, beautiful, how did you get into Heaven?

Waitress: I thought you knew, sweetie--It must have been <u>Your</u> letter of recommendation. I'd guess the guys in charge of admission to Heaven didn't want you to completely ruin the neighborhood!

Waitress: What will you two gentlemen have? Yeah, and you, too, Mr. Snake.

Metatron: I think I'll have Sapphire Gin on the rocks. Make it a triple and maybe things will look better. No one is ever supposed to get depressed in Heaven.

Gabriel: Come on, Boss, things can't be that bad. Snake and I have been down on Earth several times. Snake was in the Garden of Eden. Once he got into Heaven he didn't have to crawl on his belly. It must have been really tiring having to get around like that. You sent me down to Earth to meet up with Noah, Abraham, Jacob and Moses. They seemed to be nice fellows. Their wives were nice, too, but a little too serious.

Mr. Snake: Yeah, women can really be tough when they make up their minds. Women have caused me nothing but trouble ever since I first got involved with them. That Eve is something else. Every time I run across her in Heaven, she has fire in her eyes.

Gabriel: All the men were great family men, but the women were really the ones who kept the family traditions going. Things really came to a head when Sarah tossed out Hagar. Abraham only wanted to keep the family together. After Abraham and Sarah, Rebecca made sure about Isaac when he was getting old and a little senile. Nice girls like her, just don't do things like that. To maintain the family traditions, she really had a very good reason for picking the son who could carry on with God's wishes for Mankind. Rachel is revered as the Mother of the Israelites. Through the generations from Sarah, to Rebecca, to Rachel and Leah, the women made sure that true Spirituality that joins Man to God is continued and the men are sent to the Synagogues to study and pray. That keeps the men busy so they don't get in the way.

Metatron: Look, Gab, your talking only about the progeny of just one family and the converts who came to understand God's message of True Spirituality. But through all of the generations of

9

Man, they make up only a tiny segment of Mankind. Just a few out of the thousands of millions of people. Their understanding of God's wishes for Mankind have been rarely accepted, or if it were, God's wishes are lost in all kinds of rituals and reinterpretations. True Spirituality is more than just the belief that God is One. If it weren't so pathetic, it would really be a joke.

Waitress: Before you get too serious, fellows. How about giving me your drink orders.

Gabriel: I'll have a Southern Comfort - go easy on the mix.

Mr. Snake: Make mine Whiskey with a Beer chaser.

The two piano players have finished their raucous music and are now playing soft melodious music.

Gabriel: Give us some idea about what is troubling you, Boss.

Metatron: OK, let's start with the Garden of Eden and Mr. Snake here. God commanded Man to be fruitful and multiply. Let's start with the cardinal penalty of Eve eating from the Tree of Knowledge. Eve and all women who followed were sentenced to have excruciating pain with childbirth. The way women scream and holler at delivery, you would think that this penalty would slow things down. Oh, no, now there are so many people on Earth that there is no place for any other animals to live. The other animals are imprisoned in areas called Zoos. Millions of men and women are threatened with death from starvation but the population explosion continues.

Mr. Snake: I've followed Mankind since the beginning, and that's nothing new. People have been starving for centuries on Earth. There is one area called Africa where millions of people are threatened with starvation almost every year. Then the weather improves or faceless humanitarians come forward to feed them.

Metatron: I don't think you two really appreciate how serious things really are on Earth. God had given them the pathway to good living and even an interpretation that all men can understand. They don't need all those religions, faiths, myths, idols, "Messiahs", or soothsayers. God is troubled that so few understand. Everything is going so badly that he wants to end it all on Earth. I was appointed by God to oversee the visible Universe. By God's decree, Creation was only for Man. If Mankind no longer existed, what would be the use of it all? Besides, I could be out of a job.

Gabriel: God must have really ruffled your feathers. Boss, maybe we can work things out so God will change his mind and Men on Earth will have what they call - "Enlightenment". He's been convinced before to change his mind. Maybe He will do it again.

Metatron: Fat chance!

Mr. Snake: Gab, that's really a very tall order. Ever since God gave Man "free will" and "opened his eyes", Man's imagination has been running rampant. They think that they can understand Creation and even make the stuff of Life. I really believe that they should finally appreciate that

they are still only men. Let's take the last two hundreds of years on earth. Before then, all men lived almost the same way for thousands of years. Since the so-called "Industrial Revolution", Man's inventiveness has almost exploded with useful ideas and inventions. Horses were replaced by automobiles and trucks to carry men and materials. Vast amounts of useful energy came from "fossils" fuels. Even women's work in the home was made almost miraculously easier with all kinds of appliances both big and small. But still, with all of these wonderful achievements Man turned his inventiveness into ways to wage war. Now, these wars are waged around the entire World. Millions of men, women and children are killed. It may very well be, Mankind will end it all himself. It makes one really wonder about Mankind.

Metatron: Now you guys are beginning to understand the problems. I can't think of one area where Man has accomplished any lasting good. In the years passed on Earth, Noah, Abraham, and Moses have convinced God not to destroy Men or Mankind, but I'm afraid this will no longer be possible.

After hesitating for a few seconds -

Metatron: What do you think of this idea that might just impress God not to call everything off?

Gabriel: What's your idea? Do you think repentance will work?

Metatron: Declarations of repentance have been the watchword of Mankind. It lasts for a few weeks and then for almost any reason whatsoever Man starts complaining and repentance is ignored.

Mr. Snake: Boy, you're really serious.

Metatron: I'll have to check with God first, but I think that Mankind should know that we are going to have a Heavenly Trial to decide whether Man should continue to exist. We can bring in all kinds of witnesses from here in Heaven and some witnesses from Hell. Gabriel, you will be the Prosecuting Attorney and Mr. Snake, you will be the Defense Attorney.

Gabriel: Say, that's a great idea but don't you have things turned around? I think that I should be the Defense Attorney and Snake, here, the Prosecuting Attorney. Everyone knows I'm the good guy and Snake's the bad guy.

Metatron: No, Snake should be the Defense Attorney. He knows all of Man's bad intentions so he will know best how to defend Mankind. Snake, understand that Man's future may well depend on you. Then, again, Mankind may change his mind and think better of you.

The three get up from the table. Mr. Snake reaches into his pocket and leaves a small tip for the waitress.

Waitress: Thanks, buddy, are you sure you can afford this? You sure know how to please a lady. You, jerk.

The scene ends with the chorus and dancers singing and dancing
   "Good Guy, Bad Guy"
   "Now we know the reasons why"
   "Angels have wings white as snow"
   "And almost all Mankind belongs below."

Act 1 Scene 3

Angel Gabriel and Mr. Snake are escorted into Metatron's offices in the Hall of Judgement by his gorgeous blonde private secretary. Mr. Snake keeps his tattooed arm firmly in his jacket pocket as his piercing eyes undress this voluptuous young woman. Even in Heaven, his mischief is still uncontrollable as his Rattlesnake tattooed arm begins extending from his sleeve toward the secretary. He suddenly pulls it back when Gabriel taps on his shoulder.

Gabriel: Snake, control yourself! This is not Elysian Café.

Metatron is now not a fun loving, friendly Cherub. He is deep in thought and deadly serious.

Metatron: God has directed me to judge Mankind at a trial here in Heaven. He has appointed Mr. Snake as the Defense Attorney and you, Gabriel, as the Prosecuting Attorney. The trial will begin in two weeks Earth time. As the court system works on Earth, each of you will present witnesses to convince the jury composed of six Seraphim and six Cherubim. The jurors know that the future of Mankind may be at stake. Your witnesses may come from Heaven or Hell. Gabriel, you may call any witnesses for the prosecution you wish. Mr. Snake, you may do the same for the defense. Each of you will have the opportunity to cross-examine each witness. Prepare your presentations with the utmost care. Do not allow your friendship here in Heaven to interfere with your case presentations.

Gabriel: That's really a new twist. Do you mean that I can call on anyone here in Heaven or in Hell? There are some really odd balls in Hell. To rephrase the expression, all of them made the Earth a "Living Hell". Where will they reside in Heaven? We don't have any prisons with solitary confinements.

Metatron: You don't have to be concerned about that. They won't even know that they are in Heaven. Yes, you can call any person who has lived on Earth.

Gabriel: This trial will be different than anything that has ever happened before. After this trial, I don't think Heaven will ever be the same. All Mankind will be judge because of those maniacs who became their leaders or those men who convinced people that they are man's only Savior or Messiah. Everyone of them, or their followers, distorted living to justify murder, assassination, pogroms and propagandized national or racial superiority. What happened in the past when God spared Mankind by the kindness and charity of a few men?

Metatron: If man had benefited by the kindness and charity of those few men, then this trial would have not been necessary. In my opinion, God is determined to find justification for the survival of Mankind. God has given Man plain and simple instructions in how best he could live on Earth. Mr. Snake, you must prove that Man will finally be awakened. His eyes must be opened to understand that God's everlasting values are gifts to him and are not to be altered even by Man's best intentions. God has laid down moral and social boundaries that cannot be expanded or changed.

Metatron continues with unchallengeable conviction.

Metatron: These boundaries are moral boundaries and are clearly spelled out. These are God's laws and cannot be modified or diluted. Man can never change God's Laws and Commandments by reasoning. At times, when circumstances on earth change, Man thinks he is more modern so now his reasoning can modify or can ignore God's commandments. Man's reasoning is always faulty when he convinces other men that they can ignore or change God's commandments.

Gabriel is determined to prove to Metatron that he is sure he will successfully prosecute this case

Gabriel: *With bravado* This will be a no brainer. I have in mind a giant roster of witnesses to prove that Man is not capable of even understanding that he has failed. It is often years after each pathetic episode in man experiences that he can finally acknowledge any degree of failure. And that's called History. He keeps on making the same mistakes over and over again. It's very doubtful that he will ever learn.

Mr. Snake: *Showing his cunning* Oh, yeah, and I have in mind arguments that should sway the jury to appreciate Man's continuous problems that may influence the jury to acquit Mankind and then perhaps God will not destroy Mankind. Ever since God expelled Man from the Garden of Eden, his life has been one of uncertainty. This may be blasphemy, but I am almost convinced that it was easy for God to make Angels, but, when he made Man, a giant Pandora's box was opened- problems after problems.

Metatron: Both of you should understand that by the rules of procedure, you will present your opening remarks. Let me repeat, the witnesses for the defense will testify first and after Mr. Snake questions them, then Gabriel will have the opportunity to question each of Snake's witnesses as he desires. After the defense rests then, Gabriel, you will present your witnesses and after questioning them, Mr. Snake may question them.

Metatron: That is all for now. Miss Darling, please escort Gabriel and Mr. Snake from my office. There is much to do with little time before the trial.

The secretary is careful to avoid being anywhere near Mr. Snake as he tries his best to confront her.

Gabriel and Mr. Snake are walking down the corridor from Metatron's office.

Mr. Snake: I see all of these gorgeous broads walking around Heaven. I've go to figure out a way to wind my arms about one of them. They don't know what they're missing.

Gabriel: Snake, why don't you cool off and just concentrate on the trial.

Mr. Snake: Are you kidding? Man, snaring women is about all I think about.

Gabriel: Just to change the subject. I wonder how the Souls will take this trial? There's going to be a lot of groaning in Heaven. I can just see the biblical Patriarchs praying in the Synagogue, hour after hour, beseeching God to spare Mankind.

Mr. Snake: Maybe so, but not the Matriarchs. They're a different breed.

Gabriel: That remains to be seen.

Mr. Snake: I don't know. Men are tough. They've had to put up with all kinds of trouble. Even the Souls who are in Heaven often had to live a lifetime of abuse. They never gave up. They stuck through all kinds of misery from war to ridicule. These enlightened men and women are the men and women the world remembers. They're the ones whom parents raise their children to emulate.

Gabriel: You know, Snake, you really do have a sentimental side.
  The scene ends with the Angel chorus singing, "Sentimentally Yours".

Act I Scene 4

Moderator: The coming trial has created an excitement in Heaven between all of the Cherubim, the Seraphim and the Souls who had been admitted to Heaven from Earth. These Souls were especially impressive to the Cherubim and Seraphim, as there were so few of them. Souls from Earth who had devoted their lives to peace, to charity, to kindness, or to welcoming a stranger had made Heaven, Heaven. They lived their lives on earth following God's commandments. There was not one King, Emperor, Pharaoh, Messiah, or Savior in Heaven. This scene opens with the Cherubim and Seraphim, milling about, fascinated by the coming trial."

The scene opens on a wide boulevard in front of the Hall of Judgement and the synagogue.

Cherub 1: Do you see what I see!

Cherub 2: What's that?

Cherub 1: Look over there at all the commotion. There's Mr. Snake surrounded by Noah, the three Biblical Patriarchs, Moses and Jesus. With his reputation on Earth it's hard to understand why they even want to be seen with him. Heaven has been quiet and serene up to now. Maybe those guys know some things about Mr. Snake that they didn't know about on Earth.

Cherub 2: My, not only are they surrounding him, but they all want to talk with him at the same time! It's almost like a pushing and shoving match trying to attract Mr. Snake's attention.

Cherub 1: It must be that they know that Mr. Snake is the Defense Attorney who will try to convince the jury that Mankind must be allowed to exist.

Cherub 2: It's hard to believe that they even will trust him. Let's get a little closer and see if we can hear what they are talking about.

Suddenly, A beautiful young lady rushes past several of the Cherubim toward Mr. Snake and the Souls trying to converse with him. She is roaring mad and screaming at the top of her voice.

Eve: Do you guys know what you are doing? He (*pointing her finger directly into Mr. Snake's face)* is the reason for my excruciating pain at childbirth! Adam and I and our children had a most idyllic life in the Garden of Eden until this bozo came into our lives. He had the most beguiling manner-he could talk the pants off of you. Don't listen to even one word he is saying.

Mr. Snake: Eve, you really don't understand. I opened your eyes to the beauty of knowledge. What good was it to always be happy without knowing sadness? No, you really have me all wrong.

Eve: *(quickly turning away)* Bullshit! You ought to have your head examined. After God made us leave the Garden of Eden, we had to build our home with no windows or doors to keep out the animals with two or four feet. We had to make ladders out of vines to climb into our home and they would break time after time. Two months ago, I fell and broke my shoulder. We had three children and had high hopes for them. To our sorrow, our son, Cain, murdered our son, Abel, and then Cain

23

left with his dog and we haven't heard from him since. Every season we have to plant seeds in that lousy soil, constantly clear the weeds during the growing season and then harvest the crops so we will have enough food for the rest of the year. I've been sad all my life. So, where's the happiness?

The four Biblical Matriarchs, Sarah, Rebecca, Rachel and Leah, along with Zipporah, Moses' wife, are smiling as they watch Eve's verbal assault on Mr. Snake.

Sarah: "We should do something about our Husbands associating with that snake in the grass. I am sure the world would be a different place if it hadn't been for him and his misleading Eve.

Rebecca: Your right! I have an idea.

Zipporah: What's your idea?

Rebecca: On Earth, the way to a man's heart was through his stomach. (*Laughing*) Let them do their own cooking. Since we make such Heavenly pleasures for our husbands, I think we should cut them off for a few Earth nights. When Jesus hears about this, he will be glad that he never married.

Rachel: (*Laughing*) Yep, we can look and act like Mermaids.

Cherubim and Seraphim singing,	*"So This Is Paradise, Ha Ha Ha"*
	"Let's give 'em Hell"
	"For a spell"
	"Yes, this is Paradise, Ha Ha Ha

The crowd of men around Mr. Snake is gesticulating with both arms, each trying to be noticed.

Abraham: Mr. Snake, you must make the jury aware that our enlightenment about the true Spirituality of Men to God. This should be stressed to the jury.

Mr. Snake: I realize that Abraham, but that may not be enough to convince the jury that Man should continue to exist. So far, few men have listened to you and your messages. They've even put them in a book, but most men haven't read or haven't the foggiest idea what the book means.

Moses: But God listened to each of us when he was ready to destroy mankind. What else can be done?

Mr. Snake: (*In his most officious demeanor*) I have some ideas that may be effective. I can't tell you about them now as I am still going over them in my mind.

Moses: Can we all be witnesses for the Defense?

Mr. Snake: (*Shrugging them off, as he leaves the stage*) I'll see if the opportunity arises at the trial.

The Patriarchs, Moses, and Noah slowly walk away discouraged that Mr. Snake paid little attention to them and head for the synagogue.

Act Two

Act 2 Scene 1

In is the day of the Heavenly trial. The Seraphim and Cherubim are scurrying about back and forth calling out to their friends.

Cherub 1: I can't wait until we hear the opening statements by Mr. Snake. Gabriel has had so much knowledge of the past years on Earth that I can't see where Mr. Snake has even a remote chance of getting Man another reprieve. I wonder who he can have testify in Man's behalf? I overheard the concerned conversations between the Biblical Patriarchs and Mr. Snake. As far as I know Mr. Snake has not even asked one of them to testify. This is very unusual since God has saved Noah from the Flood, imbued Abraham and Sarah with the true spirituality, carried this Spirituality to the next generations with Isaac and Rebecca and then with Jacob and Rachel. I realize that's not many people when there were thousands upon thousands who don't even understand where this family was coming from. I can't understand why Mr. Snake has not asked for the help of any one of them.

Cherub 2: I don't know. Mr. Snake is a very uncanny guy. He didn't object to being the Defense attorney even though the Men on Earth don't think very well of him. I'm sure he has something on his mind ever since he opened Adam and Eve's eyes to reasoning and free will. I am sure he knows what he is getting into as the Defense of Man. Perhaps Mr. Snake may approach the jury with the very notion that all the rest of mankind does even know about, let alone understand, the true Spirituality of this small family's traditions.

Cherub 1: I think your right. Do you really think that God doesn't know that his commandments were never known or understood by the rest of Mankind? Mr. Snake must be very careful if he presents this argument. It may backfire on him. This is going to be very interesting with Gabriel having all of History on his side. It won't be hard for Gabriel to convince the jury that Man does not deserve to have another chance. Mr. Snake is trying to save Mankind with only his wily mind.

Cherub 2: That's a great word, wily. It fits most defense attorneys.

Cherub 1: I was over at the "We Finally Got It Right Casino", the reformed gambler's club, and the odds are 7 to 2 in favor of Gabriel. These guys will bet on anything.

The angel chorus is singing　　　*"Right Foot, Left Foot,*
　　　　　　　　　　　　　　　"No, No, Left Foot, Right Foot"
　　　　　　　　　　　　　　　　　"You've go to get it right"
　　　　　　　　　　　　　　　"We guess the future in every fight"
　　　　　　　　　　　　　　　"Gab vs. Snake, Gab vs. Snake"
　　　　　　　　　　　　　　　　　"Rah, Rah, Rah"

Crowds of Angels are heading toward the Hall of Judgement as curiosity has filled Heaven.

Cherub 2: I have a feeling I should back the underdog. I don't know where those gamblers get their information, but the side they bet on usually wins. I can feel it in my bones. Yep, I'm betting on the underdog regardless.

Cherub 1: Are you nuts! Don't waste your money. Snake hasn't got a chance.

Every seat in the Hall of Judgement is filled. The Hall of Judgement is so spacious that it seems to have no limit in size. Metatron had already selected the jury composed of six Cherubim and six Seraphim. A processional of Cherubs lead the Jury of Angels into the Hall of Judgement.
Quiet settles in over the clamor of the Angels as they scurry to their seats as the Bailiff strikes his gavel to announce the Judge Metatron.

Bailiff: Hear Ye, Hear Ye, His Honor, Metatron!

High above the assembly a chorus of angels are singing the Biblical commandments. Their voices fill the Hall with melodious symphonic tones accompanied by the Ballet of Souls.

"You shall not recognize the gods of others!"
"You shall not make yourself a carved image of any likeness
Of that which is in the heavens above, or the Earth below
Or in the waters beneath the earth"
"You shall not prostrate yourself to them or worship them
For I am the Lord, you God."
"I shall show kindness for thousands of generations to those who love me
And observe my commandments."

There is absolute quiet as Metatron enters and sits in the Judgement Choir: All is quiet as Metatron strikes his gavel.

Metatron: God has appointed me to oversee the visible Universe. Man is the "Crown of Creation" in the visible Universe. Man has failed to understand God's commandments to bring peace and happiness into the world during each man's lifetime. Instead, there has been almost continuous turmoil on Earth. Few people appreciate or even understand the essence of the Biblical Patriarch's messages. Man has paid little or no attention to the havoc he has caused on the land, in the waters, or in the sky. During Noah's lifetime, during Abraham's lifetime, God has threatened to destroy Man. Even during Moses' lifetime, God wished to replace the Israelites. At the end of this trial, the decision of the Jury will bear heavily on Man' future.

The chorus of Angels sing almost dirge like Symphonic music.

Metatron: (*Addressing the jury*) You must always understand that God has ordered this trial. We will adjourn until tomorrow when the Defense and Prosecution will present their opening remarks. I am sure the Prosecution and the Defense will present forceful arguments. Your decision will influence God for He has ordered this trial.

Act 2 Scene 2

Interest is so high in Heaven that heated discussions between the Angels have shown definite preferences for either Gabriel for the Prosecution, or Mr. Snake for the Defense. Outside the Hall of Judgement, the Souls in Heaven are pleading with every Cherub or Seriph to spare Mankind. Two of the Cherubs were talking in the hallway leading to the assembly.

Cherub 1: I just have to get inside the Hall of Judgement. While I was walking down the Boulevard of Heaven, five of the Souls surrounded me. Each of them were trying to persuade me to intervene with the Angel Metatron. I explained that I could do nothing to help them, but they still kept coming at me. I really feel sorry for them. Do you think they feel guilty that they could do nothing about all the problems of Mankind while they lived on Earth?

Cherub 2: It's hard to figure out. I don't think any of the prophets, or even the most inspired peace loving men or women were listened to or were accepted while they lived. People seemed to be more attracted to men who have evil intentions. But I suppose you're right. They really had no power to do anything about solving the problems of the hatred and mistrust of strangers. From time to time, the Israelites were not too Kosher, either, in their faith in God and His commandments.

Cherub 1: This is going to be some trial! Let's hurry inside to hear the opening arguments between Mr. Snake for the Defense and Gabriel for the Prosecution.

While the processional is leading the jury of Cherubim and Seraphim to their Golden chairs in the Jury box, the Angels are playing a Heroic symphony.

Metatron takes his place in the Chair of Judgement and strikes his gavel for silence.

Metatron: We will now hear the opening arguments by the Defense and the Prosecution. Gabriel will you come forward and begin the deliberations.

Gabriel rises and acknowledges the permission of Metatron *to address the jury.*

Gabriel: (*addressing the jury*) This trial is without doubt the most important, the most momentous, event since Creation. God created the Universe and then God placed Man on Earth to be the Crown of Creation. God gave men the commandment to lead happy and fruitful lives. The spiritual men, and there were many of them, gave their lives to interpret and disseminate these commandments to all of the people. Throughout the history of Man these few men tried without success to make all Mankind aware of God's desires for them. There were times in the Biblical history that God forgave Man and pardoned him of his sins. Nevertheless, there has been no lasting progress toward this enlightenment which is so easily to obtain. I repeat, no lasting progress. God's commandments were rejected by most of the people and nations on Earth. Is it so difficult for man to be charitable? Is it so difficult for man to welcome the stranger in his midst? Is it so difficult for Man and nations to seek pathways to lasting peace? Is it so difficult for Man to love his family and provide for them?

The assembly of Cherubim, Seraphim and Souls is becoming increasingly restless as Gabriel presses his case. Loud moans from the Souls emanate throughout the hall.

Metatron: (*striking his gavel over and over again*) I will not tolerate any expressions from the assembly. You are here to listen to the deliberations, not to participate.

(*After a brief moment*)

Metatron: Gabriel, you may continue.

Gabriel: I would like to take a brief moment to describe the progress of Humanity over the past four or five thousand Earth years. Empires would grow rich and powerful and their armies would conquer other nations without any moral purpose. These campaigns would sap their energies and soon another Empire would conquer them. All of them professed their kings to be gods, or their rulers were "chosen" by God. They made icons or pictures that depicted God, and worshipped idols that they fashioned with their own hands. They believed every part of nature was controlled by a different god. The few families who were enlightened by God to accept true Spirituality and the importance of charity, peace and kindness, had little effect on other people who could not understand that God was not a part of their existence on Earth. Most men cannot understand that God is invisible and unknowable.

The angel chorus begins to sing lines from the 135th Psalm.
   "The idol of nations are silver and gold, human handiwork."
   "They have mouths but speak not."
   "They have eyes but see not."
   "They have ears but heed not."
   "Neither is there any breath in their mouths"
   "Like them shall their makers become, everyone who trusts in them"

Gabriel: To be brief, Man has made no lasting progress. His evil ways continue to dominate his life. That Man is the Crown of Creation completely escapes him. Doesn't Man understand that God created the visible universe for Man? Man has an unfettered imagination and inventiveness that begins as sources of good but soon his ingenuity is perverted to evil uses. Man prides himself on the culture of philosophy, literature, music, song and technology; but it is all meaningless with his lack of enlightened behavior. Man disregards the need to improve his behavior. In the last 2000 Earth years, more than half of the world have accepted the concept of Monotheism, but here, too, their concepts of Monotheism are mixed with idol worship and deities conceived by Men. (*Gabriel's voice becomes loud and forceful.*) I shall present several witness to prove that Man has failed.

Gabriel bows to Metatron and returns to his seat at the Defense table.

   Moaning is heard again throughout the Hall.

Metatron: I shall not tolerate any further expressions from the assembly.

Mr. Snake, for the Defense, you may now come forward.

Mr. Snake: Your Honor, let me begin by agreeing that Man has failed in his quest to bring peace, love and understanding to the World since his beginnings. In addition, he has failed miserably in his stewardship of the other animals, on the land, in the waters and in the sky. I shall present convincing evidence that, in spite of all his shortcomings, and there are many of them, Man should continue to live on Earth. One must believe that God's hopes that Man should have been overjoyed as the Crown of Creation, but I believe that the jury should be made aware of the forces that have driven Man. These forces are not only other men with whom they could not cope, but circumstances were beyond his control.

Let the jury be cognizant of my place in Man's world. Discounting the bad reputation I have had with Man, the overwhelming explanations for the biblical goings on in the Garden of Eden were two, knowledge and understanding. Man was now a Man and different from the Angels. He had acquired reasoning and an almost uncontrollable imagination and free will. One would expect that free will would give man the insight to recognize good and evil, but free will is much more than just that. Recognition requires both knowledge and experience. His experiences have become so complex that one man or even nations cannot understand their value.

Mr. Snake is pleased that there are murmurs of approval from the assembly which are loud enough for Metatron to bang on his gavel to silence the courtroom. He also takes note of the nodding heads in approval in the Jury box.

Mr. Snake: Let me continue. When God gave True Spirituality to Noah and the Biblical Patriarchs, the ability of these men to influence other men was very little. The lives of the Patriarch covered only about 250 Earth years and then their children were cast into slavery. They grew from 70 to well over a million in the next 400 years. Their understanding of True Spirituality was taught to them after their exodus from Egypt by Moses. It is one thing to be bound together as children of one family or to join with this family by sincere conversion, but it is another to be able to bring this spirituality to other men. I shall attempt to persuade the jury that the forces of discord of mankind were so powerful that Man has now come to this critical time. I shall only call four witnesses although there have been innumerable pious scholarly men who spent their lives in True Spirituality.

Mr. Snake nods to Metatron and returns to his seat at the Defense table.

Metatron strikes his gavel.

Metatron: We shall have a short recess.

The commotion in the Hall of Judgement began almost as soon as the recess. Seraphim and Cherubim were falling in line in favor of Mr. Snake. But outside the Hall, the Souls were congregating in groups of five or six.

Abraham: I don't think that I would ever say this, but God bless the Snake. Through all these years, I am now convinced we have misjudged him.

Soul 1: I wouldn't be in such a hurry to say that. That snake is still not as wonderful as he seems to be in this trial. He may be a shifty character.

Abraham: I don't think you understand. For over two thousand Earth years, the snake has always been the brunt of the cause of the Fall of Man. His opening argument clearly explains his advise to mankind. If there ever was an opportunity to save Mankind this time, it is his Defense of Man.

Soul 1: How times change!

Act 2 Scene 3

The scene opens as the Hall of Judgement is filled with Seraphim, Cherubim and the Souls who are seated in the back of the hall. Metatron returns to his Seat of Judgement high above the assembly.

Metatron: Let us begin our deliberations with the Defense of Man. Mr. Snake, you may call your first witness.

Mr. Snake rises from the table reserved for the Defense. He has the same cocky demeanor that befits his reputation.

Mr. Snake: Your Honor, I would like to call my first witness, Professor Montaigne, a world famous Behavioral Anthropologist.

Professor Montaigne takes the witness stand. He is a rather tall, slightly obese man dressed in the traditional robe of a university professor.

Mr. Snake: Professor, would you kindly give us an explanation of your work as a Behavioral Anthropologist.

Mr. Montaigne: The scientific fields of Anthropology, Archeology and Paleontology have developed into numerous areas of investigation. Anthropology is the study of all animals and their place in nature. Archeology explores the lives of men and women from the evidence scientists can find of their past habitations. Paleontology is the study of fossils extant from the earliest development of plants and animals. Much of our explanations for what we discover change frequently. There is often overlapping and the three fields often merge or deviate from one another.

Gabriel suddenly jumps up from his chair.

Gabriel: Who is this guy? I've never heard of him. Anyway we don't need a fast track college education.

Metatron: Mr. Snake, would you please enlighten the court. This trial is a very serious matter and cannot be distracted by matters not related to our concerns.

Mr. Snake: I beg the court to have patience as I am sure you will find Professor Montaigne's testimony valuable.

Metatron: For the moment, if this is true, you may continue your interrogation, Mr. Snake.

Mr. Snake: Professor, would you favor us with a clear explanation of Behavioral Anthropology and your particular interests? It is obvious that these areas of scientific investigation are suspect as your knowledge may change and be reinterpreted.

Professor Montaigne: My research, scientific articles, and books, if I may be so bold, are the current standards that study animal and human behavior. There are many behavioral characteristics that Man has inherited from the other animals. I do not believe that there is any other explanation to account for man's behavior.

As the years pass, I have been amazed how the biblical writings are so succinct in describing human and animal behavior in just a few short phrases. Perhaps, there are other authorities who may question the authority of Biblical writings in scientific investigations but, as the years pass, I am convinced the Biblical writings are very creditable. These short biblical phrases present us with an amazing insight. For example, Adam and Eve were ashamed to be finding that they are naked. A more in depth understanding of these words are far different from merely feeling ashamed. These few words separated man from all other animals. These few words remain our most important distinction of Mankind from other animals.

As we search through the biblical writings there are other well defined statements that distinguish Man from the other animals.

Mr. Snake: What other biblical writings are you referring to?

Professor Montaigne: "And the Lion will lie down with the Lamb." This is not just an aspiration for Peace for Mankind. In their natural state, this is very true--except when the Lion get hungry. Then the lion becomes predator and the lamb becomes the prey. This is the natural order for the survival of all animals in the wild. I use the word, wild, to refer to the entire Earth, except where there is agriculture, husbandry, or human habitation.

Mr. Snake: Are there any other such succinct statements in the biblical writings?

Professor Montaigne: Yes, there are many more of them, but one that comes quickly to mind is "Be Fruitful and Multiply". Life becomes much more complicated for Man and other animals. The lamb, and I am referring to all other animals who are prey to predatory carnivores, must multiple much more frequently than the predators. In addition, both predator and prey establish territorial boundaries wherein the dominate male mates with the females for the survival of the species. And the fight to be the dominate male begins anew with each mating season. Being separated from the natural order of Nature, Man has only natural catastrophes, drought and starvation, diseases and hatred of strangers to limit the population growth. His fertility rate is so successful that the only delay is the nine month period of gestation.

Mr. Snake: What other biblical references would be useful to our defense of Man?

Professor Montaigne: Perhaps the most important is the dominion that God gave Man to be the steward of all the plants and animals. Man is separated from the Balance of Nature that determines the successful survival of all the plants and animals. Man must recognize that every form of life is directly dependent on other plants and animals. If Man, too, is survive, he must recognize the commandments to allow the land to lay fallow every few years to enable the land to regain its vigor. This also applies to the oceans, rivers, and lakes. Great areas of the oceans must be declared free from fishing for two consecutive years out of seven. This will allow the fish population to repopulate that area. The Balance of Nature in the seas mirrors the Balance of Nature on Land.

Fish are both predators or prey. The dominion over the world by Man does not permit destruction of the Balance of Nature. Man's stewardship is an awesome responsibility.

Mr. Snake: Professor, your remarks are both helpful and admirable. Do I understand correctly that you believe if Man were to truly understand the biblical writings, he could be enlightened about his purpose on Earth?

Professor Montaigne: Yes, I do.

Mr. Snake: Thank you, for your most elucidating testimony. No more questions.

Metatron: The Prosecution may now cross examine the witness.

Gabriel approaches the witness stand. He is making gestures with his arms to emphasize his questions.

Gabriel: From your remarks, I gain the impression that Mankind has little understanding of the biblical writings. Is this true?

Professor Montaigne: I must admit that this may be true.

Gabriel: Then, as we have seen since the beginning of Mankind's separation from the other animals, that Man does not have the capacity to change his behavior. Is this true?

Professor Montaigne: No, Man has the ability to change.

Gabriel: Isn't this all conjecture on your part?

Professor Montaigne: I don't think it is conjecture. The scriptures insist on rule by law. Totalitarian rule by one individual is quite the same as the dominant male animal in every land.

Gabriel: Your testimony was certainly food for thought but your conjecture is very questionable. I would like to reserve the privilege of recalling you to the witness stand when we question the witnesses for the prosecution.
Metatron: We will have a short recess and continue the trial in two hours.

The scene changes to the hallway outside of the assembly. The Matriarchs and Eve and the Patriarchs are standing together.

Eve: See, I told you not to trust that snake. His first witness is making fools of us. And you guys think he really wants to help save Mankind.

Abraham: But this is only his first witness. We should pray to God that he knows what he is doing.

Sarah: I agree with Eve. For the rest of Eternity, you will be wearing sack cloths even here in Heaven.

Rebecca: How can you men be so dumb to trust the snake? How do you know for certain that he has not sold out Mankind to those down below. My own Father misled Jacob for many years and would have destroyed our family and its traditions.

Eve: I think we should go up and down the aisles of the Hall of Judgement and protest against Mr. Snake being the Defense Attorney to save Mankind. The Angel Metatron could have found someone else, like Maimonides, to be the Defense Attorney.

The Angel chorus sings, "Oh, so naïve
Listen to Eve
She told you so
You're so slow
No one to grieve
Listen to Eve"

The trail is ready to convene after the recess. The Souls in the back rows continue to show their agitation.

Bailiff: Order in the court! Order in the court!

Mr. Snake: Your honor I would like to call my next witness, Sigmund Freud.

The Angel Gabriel jumps up from his chair, screaming at the top of his voice

Gabriel: Who? Who?

Metatron: Gabriel, Mr. Snake can call anyone he wishes. I will not tolerate such outbursts.

Mr. Snake: Thank you, Judge. Dr. Freud would you kindly take the stand.

Dr. Freud is an elderly, short, stoop shouldered, bearded man wearing a long frock coat and pince-nez glasses. He seems overawed by the Hall of Judgement.

Mr. Snake: Dr. Freud, it is a pleasure having you with us. What is it that you do on Earth?

Dr. Freud: I am a psychoanalyst.

Mr. Snake: What exactly is a psychoanalyst?

Dr. Freud: This is a very complicated field of medicine, but I try to find out what makes troubled people tick.

Mr. Snake: As I understand it, what makes people tick is their problems. Is this one person at a time, or could it be groups of people?

Dr. Freud: It is usually one person at a time but through the years of working in this area, one can make very justifiable analyses about people in general.

Gabriel suddenly jumps up from his chair.

Gabriel: I object. What has this to do with this trial?

Metatron: Objection overruled! Gabriel just sit down and listen to what Dr. Freud has to say. I am very interested.

Mr. Snake: Dr. Freud, I understand that you are the Father of Psychoanalysis. What conclusions have you drawn about Mankind?

Dr. Freud: It may seem strange to most, but Man has many problems and many of them stem from the obvious fact that he is an animal.

Mr. Snake: Why is that?

Dr. Freud: All animals have what we call animal drives and animal instincts. There are several that man has "inherited" from his animal past. One of the most important is that he is aggressive to the point where he will establish nations whose primary objective is to conquer and subjugate other people and other nations. This aggression is quite the same as predatory animals, but Man's intentions are different. Man has free will that other animals have little of.
    Predatory animals have inborn drives to establish boundaries where no other males may enter without a fight. This fight is often to the death. This instinct is to guarantee, by his strength and cunning, the survival of his progeny from problems each future generation may encounter. As Professor Montaigne testified, "The Lion will lie down with the Lamb" when he is not hungry. But not man. He will continue to be aggressive almost without reason. Nations of men will start wars over even the smallest piece of territory that they have declared as theirs. These nations of men claim superiority over other nations or other men. I have never been a religious man, but almost all nations have little appreciation of kindness or charity toward anyone or any nation different from themselves.

Mr. Snake: Dr. Freud, are there any other instincts that man has that are also animal instincts?

Dr. Freud: Yes, I believe that the domination by a single male may be the reason for mankind to allow one-man rule. The "Devine Right of Kings" so common for centuries, the absolute rule by emperors, and the willingness to accede to Dictatorships are all derived from animal instincts-the herd is subservient to the dominate Male. All other males are chased away or are killed by the dominate male.

All of the Souls in the rear of the assembly suddenly stand up.

Souls: We want to be heard! We want to be heard!

Metatron: Souls, if Mr. Snake wants to hear from you, he will call you to the witness stand. If you want to stay in the Hall, sit down!

Mr. Snake: Do you think that given enough time Man can change for the better?

Dr. Freud: I am sure this is possible.

Mr. Snake: Then what do you think can be done?

Mr. Freud: It has already been done. When Man discovered he could rule by laws, dramatic changes took place in the world. These rules by law were first embraced by only by a small group of men and women. This insight to rule by laws instead of one king or dictator could only have come from those people who understood and accepted true Spirituality. One might say that, with the recognition of the true spirituality, these small number of people psychologically had become a different species from the rest of Humanity. Psychologically, they have become a mutation from the rest of Mankind.

Mr. Snake: Do you honestly believe that psychologically they are a different species of Mankind?

Dr. Freud: Their transformation is proven, because those men and women, and their converts, have replaced aggression with understanding true Spirituality with peace, charity, and good will toward others. This instinct is so powerful that thousands and thousands of their followers have been slaughtered through the centuries without changing their convictions. I must emphasize that this radical suppression of basic animal instincts is not merely confined to this small group, but it becomes the way of life for converts as well.

Mr. Snake: Hasn't this change in instincts impressed the others?

Dr. Freud: I'm afraid not. The forces opposing this mutation from the rest of Humanity are overwhelming. Hatred for strangers have been the watchwords for the rest of Humanity. Hand in hand with Man's continuing aggressions is Polytheism. Polytheism's belief in idols and the acceptance of the supernatural continues to be so deeply entrenched that most people are convinced these idols dominate their actions and feelings. Their gods of war define their convictions.

Mr. Snake: What about the religions that profess Monotheism?

Dr. Freud: Without their realization, the retention of their convictions about the supernatural such as the implied deity of men who have lived on Earth or men who have become godlike, prevent acceptance of peace, charity and good will. These convictions continue to perpetuate their aggressions. There is little place for the understanding of the true relationship between God and Man. Monotheistic religions give God-like attributes to men who are mortal like Jesus arising from the dead or Mohammed riding horse up to Heaven.

The angel chorus repeats the 135th Psalm.

Mr. Snake: Thank you, Mr. Freud. You have presented to the jury the explanation for the overwhelming, poorly understood, problems of Mankind and the solution for their future survival. I sincerely believe that Man needs more time to reach this enlightenment.

The souls cannot restrain themselves and continue applauding Mr. Freud, shouting and racing up and down the aisles of the Hall.

Metatron: (Striking his gavel repeatedly) I have had enough of your demonstrations! Clear the hall of all Souls!

After all of the Souls have left the Hall of Judgement, the trial continues.

Metatron: The prosecution may begin the cross-examination.

The Angel Gabriel approaches the Witness Stand walking back and forth in front of Freud.

Gabriel: Mr. Freud, or let me address you properly as Doctor Freud, that was a most impressive dissertation about Mankind. Let me ask you, don't you think it is far fetched to explain the course of Humanity through thousands of years because he is only an animal?

Dr. Freud: Let me explain.

Gabriel: Please answer, Yes or No.

Dr. Freud: But, But-

Metatron: Answer the prosecutor.

Dr. Freud: (*Obviously, emotionally disturbed*) Well, Yes.

Gabriel: Don't you realize that Man, however tarnished, is the crown of Creation. God gave man so much more than animals that there is really little comparison. Animals live from one generation to another the same as the previous generation. They are born, spend their lives, reproduce and die with no spiritual manifestations whatsoever. There is the comic comparison, "They may look like a duck, walk like a duck, but man is not a duck! How can you declare God's gifts of Free Will, reasoning, and even his imagination to be inconsequential?

Dr. Freud: I did not say they were inconsequential. I claim they are always dominated by animal drives and instincts.

Gabriel: Even if you are correct, does not that prove Mankind is hopeless in wanting another chance?

Dr. Freud: With those few followers of True Spirituality, men and women and their converts who have this psychological mutation will give Mankind another chance to recognize and follow True Spirituality.

Gabriel: It didn't work several times before, Man's degradation is so much deeper now than in the past, I think Man has had his last chance. No more questions.

Metatron: Thank you, Doctor Freud. You may step down.

Metatron: We will now recess until tomorrow afternoon when the Defense will present its next witness.

The assembly of Cherubim and Seraphim quickly join in heated discussions.

Cherub 1: "I can't wait until tomorrow. I think Mr. Snake is winning his case so far."

Cherub 2: "I don't know. The Angel Gabriel has a mountain of evidence against man that man has no chance to exist any longer."

Cherub 1: "I kind of like Man. I, myself, think he is irreplaceable. I'm sure God will give Man another chance."

Cherub 2: If you are right, Man better accept the True Spirituality of that little group of men and women. And Man better do it soon."

Act 2 Scene 4

It is almost noon the next day. The piazza in front of the Hall is crowded with Angels waiting to get a seat for the trial. Mr. Snake is making his way to the Hall of Judgement when he hears-

Biblical Matriarchs: Hey Snake, cum' on over here.

Mr. Snake turns toward four lovely young ladies who are beckoning him with their body language. Nothing was ever so enticing to Mr. Snake. In a fast pace, with a glint in his eyes, he walks over to them.

Mr. Snake: Is there anything I can do for you? Anything?

Matriarch Sarah: You bet. We think we can help you if you will spend a little time with us.

Mr. Snake, drooling at the mouth with anticipation, and thinking if he could only get them one at a time.

Mr. Snake: The trial begins soon but it should be over in a few hours. Then we can meet at the Elysian. How about early this evening?

Matriarch Sarah: That will be fine but we wanted to talk with you about this prosecutor, Gabriel. I knew him when Abraham brought him and his buddies into our tent. The problem is that Abraham does the inviting and I do all the work. I had to clean the tent, slaughter and dress the lamb, make the fire, roast the lamb, roast some potatoes, and set the table. Thank god, I made the Challah yesterday. It was so damned hot that day that I thought I would fall over. All Abraham, Gabriel and his friends did was drink wine and shoot the breeze. Then I had to bow down to them and, with my sweetest smile, invite them to the table. We're convinced the world would be better if women ran the place.

Mr. Snake: But how can that help me with the trial?

Matriarch Sarah: I think this is important. The Angel Gabriel never really wanted to be the Prosecuting Attorney against Mankind. He came to us to judge Abraham's sincerity. I am sure he reported to Metatron that he was convinced that Abraham could lead the world toward True Spirituality. Eventually, sometime during the trial, Gabriel will show his true love of Mankind, and the case for the prosecution will cave in.

Mr. Snake: You may be right about Gabriel not wanting to be the Prosecutor but Metatron insisted. When we met the next day in Metatron's office, God had agreed on this arrangement. But I think we are on the same page in our thoughts about women. They are tough. I should know with Eve always breathing down my neck here in Heaven. I'm not so sure women should run the world, but, again, they probably couldn't do it worse that the men. I hope you will be pleased to know that my next witness is a woman.

The Biblical Matriarchs: Who will she be?

Mr. Snake: I can't tell you now but if you will be allowed to go into the Hall of Judgement after yesterday demonstrations by the Souls, I think you will be pleased. How about the Elysian?

The Biblical Matriarchs: You do a good job, one of us will be there in our finest. Knowing you, you will be delighted. It will be something special.

Mr. Snake: What so special?

Matriarch Sarah: We decided that the lady picked to meet you won't be completely dressed. What would you like her to be missing?

Mr. Snake: No panties?

Matriarch Sarah: How did you guess? Mr. Snake, you rascal, you really know women.

Mr. Snake: Am I right?

Sarah smiles and throws him a kiss.

Suddenly the Snake's tattooed rattlesnake arm extends as stiff as an erection. Mr. Snake smacks his arm with the other trying to get it to relax as he is about to enter the Hall of Judgement.

Mr. Snake feels lasciviously triumphant. Looking at his watch.

Mr. Snake: I better get to the trial. It's getting late and Metatron will be plenty sore if I'm late.

Act 2 Scene 5

The Hall of Judgement is overflowing with Angels and Souls. At the last moment before Metatron enters, Mr. Snake rushes in toward the Defense table still smacking his tattooed arm trying to get it to relax.

Bailiff: Hear Ye, Hear Ye, His Honor Metatron.

Complete silence comes over the assembly. Gabriel is standing before the prosecution table and Mr. Snake is before the Defense table.

Metatron enters and takes his place high above the assembly.

Metatron: We are about to begin today's deliberations. I will not tolerate outbursts of any kind from the assembly such as occurred yesterday. The Defense may call its next witness.

Mr. Snake: I wish to call my next witness, Abigail Adams.

Gabriel suddenly jumps up from his chair, stares at the judge, and then decides not to interfere with the proceedings, and sits down.

Abigail is a matronly woman, with a self-assured demeanor, dressed in the fashion of the American revolutionary period.

Mr. Snake: Mrs. Adams, may I call you by your first name, Abigail?

Abigail: Please, do.

Mr. Snake: Abigail, let me review the circumstances that made me confidant that you could help the defense. As you know, Man's future existence is on trial. We have always been impressed by the radical change in the affairs of man that resulted in the American Revolution and the desires of the American people to live in a law abiding society without kings or any other kinds of totalitarian rule. This had never been done before. You have been a great student of history, as well as being very instrumental in the political affairs of this new, and let me say, original concept of government. Would you kindly give us your feelings about history that may help us save Mankind.

Abigail: I want to thank you for your flattery, and I hope I will be able to influence the jury. There are two impressions I have carried for many years. One is the problem that has confronted men since time immemorial and the other is surprisingly how perceptive my thoughts have been for the future of women. "God knows", the world needs a "Mother's touch". I am a Christian woman but the words of the Bible concerning Noah's sons have always embittered me. That one son should serve another does not mean that one son should be the slave of the other sons. It is an inheritance through the centuries from ancient polytheistic religions and an expression of man's aggressiveness to conquer, subdue or kill. In my lifetime, a black man is enslaved just because he is black is an unconscionable travesty. Since time immemorial, men have satisfied their bestial instincts by the chattel of men and women. For the male leaders of all religions, they must realize,

this is a sin. No man should ever be the property of another. To free our country of this terrible burden because of this misconstrued Biblical interpretation, millions of our citizens would die in the Civil War.

Mr. Snake: Abigail, let me interrupt you for a moment. Then you feel that Man is capable of finally recognizing his errors against his fellow men. Is this the sense of what you are saying?

Abigail: This is surely true. If Man has Free Will, he can use it constructively rather than use free will to perpetuate his aggressiveness. Once our government of the people was established, it took only 60 years in America to correct the horrors of slavery that have haunted history for thousands of years.

Mr. Snake is smiles inwardly as he is certain that her words are impressing the jury. In the back of the assembly, the Souls are almost unable to constrain themselves.

As if on cue, the angel chorus begins to sing,
   "Bondage is the Swamp of Ages:
   "The fire of pain and injustice rages"
   "What so seals a man's fate"
   "The day is falling, oh so late"
   "Bring forth hope, bring back hope"

Metatron: Abigail, you may step down for a few minutes and we will resume after a 30 minute recess.

In the back of the hall, Noah, Abraham, Moses, and the other Matriarchs are shouting and waving their arms.

Moses: Now I know why we are unable to make a lasting impression on anyone.

Abraham: Don't be so hard on yourself.

Moses: I'm sure our mistake has been to set ourselves up as paragons of virtue. Instead, we should have made our followers and all other men aware that Men had to change from their "basic" animal instincts. These instincts drive their aggressiveness to other men. Man must recognize the necessity for ridding themselves of these instincts. Kindness, charity and peace escapes them, but this is what God wanted for them. This was our mission and we failed in not understanding this.

Abraham: Do you think that this mistake includes Jesus?

Moses: In his way, he continued making our mistake.

Abraham: How about Mohammad?

Moses: He's another story. I am sure he nurtured Man's aggressiveness. This nurturing allowed this religion to spread across the world in only a few years. There was nothing to stop them. His followers were unwilling to change their aggressiveness. They never had any intention of changing their animal instincts.

Abraham: That woman, Abigail, she's a splitting image of our wives. I wonder how women have so much perception?

Moses: Let's admit it. They have a gift from God.

The blast of a Ram's horn sounds. The deliberations are about to begin again.

Metatron strikes his gavel.

Metatron: The trial will now proceed. Abigail, will you kindly return to the witness stand.

Mr. Snake walks confidently toward the witness stand half facing the jury and half toward the witness stand.

Mr. Snake: Abigail, surely your testimony will prove to the jury that Mankind can benefit by his Free Will. Then he will recognize all the bestial thoughts and actions he takes are because of his inherited instincts. Then we pray that the jury's verdict will be give Man at least one more chance. Will you proceed on to your second impression.

Abigail: The abolition of slavery clearly demonstrated that Man has the capacity to reason and to move beyond his instincts of aggression and predatory behavior. The second suggestion is more subtle. Mankind must unshackle bondage of women. Since time immemorial, Mankind has suppressed women. It is men who have lascivious behavior, not women. It is men who have demeaned the intelligence of women. Has not the contributions of our Biblical Matriarchs made them understand that God endowed women with the qualities to perpetuate Kindness, Peace and Charity? Yes, the Biblical Patriarchs were great family men, but it is their wives who were endowed with carrying forth the precepts of Kindness, Peace and Charity to future generations. Their progeny and the many people who convert, for the most part, have suppressed the innate aggressiveness of Mankind. I am proud to say that, after me, have come many many women who continue to unshackle the bonds imposed on women. For this reason, too, Mankind should have another chance.

Mr. Snake: Abigail, I could not have chosen a better person to prove to the jury that Mankind needs another chance.

Metatron: The Prosecution may now cross-examine the witness.

Gabriel: "No…….No Questions."

Metatron: Mr. Snake, you may now call your next witness.

Mr. Snake: Your Honor, I would like to call my fourth and last witness, Professor Albert Einstein.

Professor Einstein is dressed in Victorian fashion. It is difficult to judge his height as he is now stooped over in his latter years. He has a full head of grew hair with still a sparkle in his eyes.

Metatron: You have no equal in all the history of Man in the science of Theoretical Physics. In addition, the past three hundred years on Earth has surpassed all of the knowledge of technology and inventions of men since the beginning of time. It is our pleasure to have you testify at this trial. Please take the stand.

The Angel chorus begins to sing: *"He's Our Boy"*
                                            "He's Our Boy"
                                            "He knows time, he knows space"
                                            "He even knows the human race."

Mr. Snake is as proud as a Peacock as he approaches the witness stand. The remark by Metatron emphasized the importance of this witness to the trial.

Mr. Snake: I have selected only four witnesses to testify in the behalf of Man. In your lifetime, Man has been confronted by wars, pestilence, and starvation such has been never known before. As the defenders of Mankind, there is little that may justify Man's continued existence other than the opinions of Dr. Montaigne, Sigmund Freud, Abigail Adams, and you. What are your impressions on the fate of Mankind?

Professor Einstein: Yes, I have lived to witness the horrors perpetrated by my generation of men. However, there is a new threat. Man has now the capability to totally destroy himself without God's help. My life and thoughts have only been directed toward the Peace, Charity, and Good Will, but there are men of science who, for whatever their reasons, pervert peaceful invention and innovation toward the destruction of Mankind.

In the latter years of my life, as you know, I was forced to abandon my country and settle in America. As I look back, how could so rich and powerful a nation allow its leadership to be guided by a maniacal dictator. I am sure their citizens were driven by their bestial instincts. They gave little thought to the evils expressed in concentration camps that massacred millions of innocent men, women and children.

Were one to question me about the development of my theoretical analyses of the vast amount of energy contained in radioactive material, I would still unquestionably approve of making the atomic bomb as this maniac would have progressively turned humanity back into an irrecoverable "Dark Age". He and his allies had to be stopped at any cost. No, members of the jury, peace can only be perpetuated by fighting against such evils. God willing, He will give Mankind another chance to make our Earth into the World that He wished us to be. We must understand that we are not animals with uncontrollable drives and instincts. Yes, we are animals, but we are animals who can have the will to seek peace with our fellow men.

Mr. Snake: Professor Einstein, do you have other thoughts about your contribution to Theoretical Physics?

Professor Einstein: The world's need for energy has increased many times since the Industrial Revolution. The development of using atomic power for peaceful purposes would fulfill this need. One atomic facility could replace mining millions of toms of coal whose electric plants pollute the environment, poison the air we breathe, and "break men's backs". If God were to give us another chance, we have the capacity and knowledge to make a New World.

Mr. Snake: Thank you, Professor Einstein. No more questions.

Metatron: The Prosecution may cross-examine the Witness.

Gabriel approaches the witness stand with a confidence that he can persuade the jury.

Gabriel: This trial has been called to demonstrate that Mankind may not deserve to continue to exist. Don't all the facts of life convince you that Man is headed toward self-destruction even without God's command?

Professor Einstein: No, Man has the means to refine his role in our World.
Gabriel: Let us go back in time three hundred years or so before the Industrial Revolution. Has there ever been a generation of men who could change life for the better?

Professor Einstein: No.

Gabriel: Now we are getting some place. Man's has existed for thousands of generations and has never even come close to any enlightenment. Isn't this true?

Professor Einstein: No, I believe you must qualify the term enlightenment. Admittedly there has been only one tiny group of people and their proselytes who have given Mankind God's message of peace, kindness and charity. Although they have been constantly persecuted, they persist against all odds to cherish God's commandments for how to live their lives, and the lives of all other men and women, with the greatest expectations for happiness, good health, and personal achievement.

Gabriel: But no one listens, not even most of their adherents. Don't you think this is a dying cause?

Professor Einstein: No, we must have hope.

Gabriel: Phooey, no more questions.

Professor Einstein leaves the witness stand looking for some help from Mr. Snake, obviously troubled by the cross-examination.

Metatron: It has been a long day. We will reconvene tomorrow when the Prosecution will present their witnesses.

Act Three

Act 3 Scene 1

The scene opens in the hall leading into the Hall of Judgement. Mr. Snake is looking furtively in the hall and outside in the piazza for the lovely young ladies who had promised him intimate relations with one of them. It is almost time for the trial to commerce but Mr. Snake still persists in looking for them. A promise is a promise. He is finally beginning to realize that his idea of this promise is nothing but a promise.

Gabriel: Hey, Snake! What are you doing running in and out of the building? I'd like to talk to you about the trial.

Mr. Snake finally gives up his quest and walks over to Gabriel.

Mr. Snake: Yeah, what is it you wanted to talk about?

Gabriel: I just wanted to congratulate you on your defense yesterday. Boy! You must have had to dig pretty deep to find your witnesses. That Abigail Adams was something else. I was thinking out of a sense of fairness, since you only called four witnesses, I might do the same. I really don't have to dig too deep, I had hundreds of possible witnesses to prove that Mankind is falling over the edge. Four witnesses should be more than enough.

Mr. Snake: I am sure you will have an easy time finding witnesses for the Prosecution, but I'm sure the jury got my message. I understand you went to see the judge last night. What was that all about?

Gabriel: Oh, I just wanted to bring a couple of my buddies to join the Prosecution and get their advice during the trial. You know, the other two who also visited Abraham in his tent. Metatron Ok'ed it.

Mr. Snake: What's the matter, aren't you confident in yourself?

Gabriel: As I told you before, this is a no brainer. I just want you to feel lonely all by yourself at the Defense table.

Mr. Snake: That's a laugh. I've always been by myself. Say, who are your four witnesses?

Gabriel: What do you think this is? This trial is in Heaven. It's not like trials on Earth. You will see my witnesses as they take the stand.

In another part of the hall are the Three Patriarchs, Moses, and Noah.

Abraham: I suppose Gabriel will really be laying it to us when the Prosecution presents its case against Mankind.

Moses: You may be right, but when God wanted to get rid of the Israelites after the Exodus from Egypt. I persuaded him to change his mind. It didn't take much of an appeal from me. We have a very compassionate God.

Noah: That's true. He decided to save me and my family from the Flood, and I wasn't even Jewish.

Abraham: I really believe that Mr. Snake has made a very strong argument to give Mankind another chance. It may be that at creation of Man, God had to start out with some really defective material. The natural world was designed to work like a smooth running operation. Man just doesn't fit in.

Moses: I hope the jury will be as compassionate. As I understand it, juries just examine the facts and I fear compassion is not allowed to be considered. Well, let's go in to hear the prosecution and pray that Gabriel will not be too severe on Mankind.

Abraham: Say, what's going around over there?

In the distance, at the edge of the piazza, a troop of soldiers with bright bronze spears and bronze breastplates and shining helmets, are marching back and forth with exaggerated goose steps. After several intricate formations, they suddenly align their rows and begin a steady march toward the entrance to the Hall of Judgement.

Moses: I don't know, but we better go into the hall before they get here.

Act 3 Scene 2

The Hall of Judgement is filled with Seraphim, Cherubim and Souls waiting quietly for the trial to continue. Metatron enters the chamber high above the assembly.

Bailiff: The trial will now come to order. His Honor, Metatron presiding.

Metatron: The Defense has presented its witnesses and the Prosecution has cross-examined them. We will now proceed with the Witnesses for the Prosecution. Angel Gabriel you may begin.

Gabriel: For my first witness I call the King of Moab.

The doors of the Hall of Judgement open widely and in march the troop of soldiers smartly goose-stepping to the rhythm of drums and horns. In the center of the lines of soldiers in a platform held high by eight of the soldiers. Seated in his throne on the platform, dressed in gold adornments, and scarlet and purple clothes is the King of Moab, Golden spear in hand. Commanding officer. Company, Halt!

The platform is slowly lowered as the soldiers gradually kneel reverently to the ground. The King of Moab rises and struts toward the Witness Stand.

Metatron: King of Moab would you kindly take the stand, and send your soldiers out of the Hall. This is not a circus.

The commander of the troop raises his sword, and the troop comes to attention. The horns and drums blast forth and the troop marches goose-stepping out of the Hall of Judgement.

Gabriel: King, tell us about yourself.

King: It should be obvious to everyone that I am the King of the great country of Moab. My faithful soldiers, led by my stalwart commanders, have conquered city-state after city-state. We are born and bred to fight wars. My men follow me into battle and we are always successful. Those soldiers of our enemies who are not killed in battle are forced into slavery for our benefit. Their women also serve us in many ways. If you know what I mean.

Gabriel: Don't these city-states have kings and royalty?

King: Certainly, a few of the royal families are able to escape but most of the time when they are captured, they plead for mercy. We have festivals to send these royal families into the never never land. This way, our enemy royal families and their loyal subjects don't cause us any more trouble.

Gabriel: What would happen if you were not successful in every battle?

King: That, my friend, will never happen. I will never be defeated.

Gabriel: That's what I call confidence. Tell me, do the people of Moab have a religion?

King: I am the god of Moab. Of course, we also worship the Sun, the Moon, and our holy mountain, but I am the God of War, the supreme god.

Gabriel: How did you become god?

King: Our high priests have declared me, god. Our high priests tend the magnificent statue of me in the city center, supervise the festivals, pronounce who shall live and who shall die. All traitors die. They are also very careful to insure the obedience of the people of Moab to me.

Gabriel: That is very interesting. How does one become a High Priest?

King: I appoint the High Priests.

Gabriel: Tell me King, have you ever hear of Abraham?

King: Abraham, Abraham? Do you mean that screwball up North who believes in an invisible god?

Gabriel: Yes, that's him.

The King of Moab suddenly stands, strikes his spear and then raises it.

King: He doesn't understand anything about this world. Power is everything. You must conquer or be conquered. Every man and woman and child must completely support the state without reservation. There is no room for anything else.

Gabriel: Are you familiar with him?

King: Yes, I met him a couple of times when I wanted to get some idea of the strength of his army. He tried to make me understand the importance of welcoming a stranger. Well, we do welcome strangers. We welcome them into our city and give them a bed. If they are too short for the bed we stretch them. If they are too tall for the bed, we chop off their feet to fit the bed. Spies are a big trouble.

Gabriel: Do you think that is the way things should be?

King: (*Leaning forward and glowering intensely and shouting at Gabriel*) This is the way men will always be ruled.

Gabriel: Then you don't think that Man can even understand Abraham's concept of an Invisible God and God's directions for way men should treat his fellow men.

King: No way.

Gabriel: No more questions.

Metatron: The Defense may now cross-examine the witness.

Mr. Snake walks back and forth in front of the witness stand.

Mr. Snake: Those are really fancy Royal robes, King.

King: (*Obviously pleased*) It took almost a year for my skilled tailors to design them. Pretty neat, eh?

Mr. Snake: Why are you so convinced that the world of men will never get any better?

King: Look, Junior, I also have had the opportunity to see what has been going on Earth since I left. I know that you definitely do not approve of me. But we have a number of Souls down where I come from who have copied me. They were really something while they lived on Earth. And that was only a few years ago. If you think that I was ruthless, just compare me to Stalin who killed a few million and Hitler who takes the cake-over 40 Million! If he hadn't made the mistake of murdering six million of Abraham's following, he might be still doing his stuff.

Mr. Snake: I am sure you are aware that almost half of the people of the world have embraced the concept of one God and that God demands that he should not be represent by anything on Earth. No idols, no kings, no soothsayers, no one can have any conception of God. He has also given Man the pathways to reaching good health, happiness for each man's family, and charity and kindness to other men. What are your thoughts about that?

King: Are you kidding? I don't think that most of them even give a thought to what you call "God's Commandments". They're more interested in bowing down to their leaders or agreeing that they must protect or expand their territory. I'm telling you, the world will never change.

Mr. Snake: No more questions.

After the questioning of the King of Moab, the doors of the assembly swing open and King Moab's goose-stepping troops come marching in with their drums beating and horns blowing. They bow to the King and carry him seated on his throne, raise the platform, and carry him out.

As soon as the King of Moab leaves the hall, the Souls begin their lament
  "Oey Vey, What a Day!"
  "The world is going the other way."
  "Change our mourning into dancing"
  "Dear God, have mercy on our world."

After a rather lengthy admonition for quiet by the Bailiff, the trial recommences.

Metatron: Gabriel, you may call your next witness.

Gabriel: My next witness is not well known in history except perhaps as a writer-philosopher during the tumultuous times of the Italians in the 14ᵗʰ and 15ᵗʰ centuries. Like Moab, this land filled with city-states, all at odds with one another, all at odds with the Papacy in Rome and each threatened by the aggressive designs of France, Spain and Germany. I now call to the witness stand Niccolo Machiavelli.

Machiavelli walks hesitantly toward the witness stand. He is absolutely stunned by the magnificence of the Hall of Judgement. He appears uncertain as to why or what he is doing here.

Gabriel: Senore Machiavelli, I want to welcome you.

Machiavelli pays little attention to Gabriel as he looks from right to left, up and down, and back to right to left in wonderment. He begins speaking in a heavy Italian-American accent.

Machiavelli: What's a this a place?

Gabriel: This' a place is the Hall of Judgement.

Machiavelli: Oh, what's a you want from me? I ain't done not'tin wrong. Maybe you got'ta me confused with someone else'a..

Gabriel: No, Niccolo, no one else.

Machiavelli: You sure?

Gabriel: I'm sure. I believe you can help us. We are having a trial here in Heaven to try to decide whether Mankind should continue to exist.

Machiavelli: But I'm'a just a simple man. I live'a simple life.

Gabriel: Have you ever heard of the land of Moab?

Machiavelli: No, it doesn't even sound Italian.

Gabriel: About 3500 years ago there was a land of Moab. Interestingly enough in the time of Moab, the country was filled with city-states much like your country. And much like your country, these city-states were always at war with one another.

Machiavelli: You don't say. Dat long ago?

Gabriel: Yes, that long ago.

Gabriel: You wrote a principle in one of your articles that I would like to quote. "The world has been inhabited by human beings who have the same passions." Could you expand on that principle?

Machiavelli straightens in his chair and assumes an entirely different composure than the frightened little Italian.

Machiavelli: I hope you will excuse my little charade but one cannot be too careful. When I was a young man, your future success in life had to be with royalty or to be sponsored by a wealthy influential family. I had neither. I had to educate myself and I carefully paid attention to the political affairs of royal families and the influential families I served under. I wrote many articles and books giving advice to my superiors about politics and how to survive the ambitions and intrigue of other nations. The most outstanding was my book, "The Prince". But the basis of almost all my writings was that quote. Mankind has the same passions throughout history. Power breeds hate, deceit and intrigue. What seems white in the affairs of government is in reality black and vis versa. Innocent people are tortured until they falsely confess and then they are murdered. This was the world I lived in.

Gabriel: That's an overwhelming condemnation.

Machiavelli: From what you tell me, that's the way it was, that's the way it was in my days, and that's the way it will probably be in the future. Nothing will ever change.

Gabriel: You rarely mentioned this, but what about the common man?

Machiavelli: Life will always be the same. No one ever cared about slaves or those poor people who had no hopes. No one in these governments cared a fig about them. Of course, we may have needed them as mercenaries in our armies, but it was paying them for their lives.

Gabriel: I understand that your allegiance was to the city-state of Florence. Is this true?

Machiavelli: Yes, I had many political and military posts. I often traveled to Germany and France as my king could not trust any other emissary. As I said, the times were filled with intrigue and deceit. My travels confirmed my impression of the futility of national alliances. There was never any intention of peace. It was just conquer or be conquered..

Gabriel: The Popes, were they men of deep religious faith?

Machiavelli: Are you kidding? They were installed as Popes by the political strength or wealth of their families. They were no different from the other kings and emperors. The Vatican controlled the politics of other nations in Europe through the power of the Papacy. The Inquisition defined the heretic as anyone not Catholic. Celibacy for the Popes was a joke but political assassination and murder were condoned.

Gabriel: Your book, "The Prince" why did you write it?

Machiavelli: A writer has either a story to tell, or he has instructions to offer. "The Prince" is a manual of instruction for heads of state. It gives them advice on how to govern in this hectic world.

Gabriel: Was it well accepted?

Machiavelli: I understand it has been a "best seller" for hundreds of years.

Gabriel: Really?

Machiavelli: As I have said before, men who inhabit the earth, all have the same passions. "The Prince" gives them instructions on how to make the best of their passions. Man will never change or think in any other way.

Gabriel: Niccolo, thank you for your testimony.

Machiavelli rises to leave the witness chair but the Bailiff motions for him to remain there. Pandemonium breaks out in the back of the hall where the Souls are seated.

The Angel chorus begins to sing
   "Put no trust in princes"
   "Mortal man can give no help."

Bailiff: (*Shouting*) Order in the court! Order in the court!

Metatron: The Defense may now cross-examine the witness.

Mr. Snake: Mister Machiavelli, have you ever been the head of a state? Have you ever ruled?

Machiavelli: No

Mr. Snake: And you lived in a tiny bit of land?

Machiavelli: Yes.

Mr. Snake: Since you have never been the head of a state or have knowledge about the rest of the world, why do you think you can draw momentous conclusions on the fate of Mankind?

Machiavelli: Perhaps not, but I still think I'm right.

Mr. Snake: Those heretics you referred to during the period of the Inquisition who were expelled from their countries or murdered, do you have any idea why they struggled against the Catholics?

Machiavelli: It was no concern of mine.

Mr. Snake: For thousands of years, they have been trying to enlighten Mankind that their bestial instincts lead only to murder, war, assassination, deceit and intrigue. Not Kings, but common men for whom the Universe was created, may soon gladly embrace Peace, Understanding and the need for Charity. These are the precepts of the future.

Gabriel suddenly stands.

Gabriel: Objection! Objection! The Defense has no right to pontificate to the witness.

Metatron: Objection sustained. Mr. Snake, you are in a courtroom. Observe the rules.

Mr. Snake: Mr. Machiavelli have you ever heard of representative government?

Machiavelli: No, What's that?

Mr. Snake: You must know that your name has come to denote a wicked person. Your instructions have carried wickedness down to the present time on Earth. Admittedly Man is threatened by his own destruction. But in the past few centuries, common man has asserted himself by affirming God's precepts on how to best live in this world. Common man is gaining by voting in men to lead him without political assassination and limiting each elected person to a period of leadership. Then the leader is replaced peacefully.

Machiavelli: That's a new twist.

Mr. Snake now feels he has blunted the testimony of Machiavelli.

Mr. Snake: I have no more questions.

As Machiavelli leaves the witness stand, the Angel chorus sings, "Hurrah for Love".

Metatron: It has been a long day. We will now recess until tomorrow when the Prosecution will continue.

Act 3 Scene 3

The Four Matriarchs and Eve were off to one side of the Piazza when Mr. Snake arrives. They are acting as if he were a stranger.

Mr. Snake: Ladies, I thought I had an agreement to meet one of you at the Elysian.

Eve: Which One?

Mr. Snake: How would you know which one? You weren't there.

Eve: Listen, Snake, why don't you wake up. I know all about it. One of those lovely ladies would have to be nuts to have anything to do with you.

Mr. Snake: Just like a woman. Your starting this harangue all over again? Let me talk with one of them. Sarah! Sarah!

The ladies all turn away as if he never existed. Mr. Snake is finally convinced that he's been had, and turns and heads for the Hall of Judgement. Meanwhile, the Patriarchs, Moses and Noah are in the Synagogue reciting every psalm in the Tehillim.

Moses: Now Psalms 2, 4, 6 and 9.

Noah: Look, at this rate we'll never get to the trial. Do you think that the more Psalms you recite, the more God will listen to you? This could go on for hours.

Moses: Just about ten more.

After about what seems to Noah to be an hour, the time for the trial is about to start

Moses: I think we should now recite Kaddish.

Noah: (*Exasperated*) What's that!

Moses: We must recite Kaddish, It's the mourner's prayer. But it has nothing to say about death. It is beautiful and was composed when our people were in Babylonia.

After reciting the Kaddish, the three Patriarchs, Moses and Noah leave the Synagogue which is to the right of the Hall of Judgement, just as the proceedings are to begin. They hurry to their seats in the last row.

Bailiff: Order in the Court, Order in the Court!

Metatron: Does the Prosecution have additional witnesses?

Gabriel: Yes, Your Honor, I wish to call Mohammad to the witness stand.

Mohammad takes the stand. He is dressed in royal Arab robes. At his waist he carries a golden scimitar and his head is covered with a turban.

Gabriel: From your life in the Arabian Desert, you certainly have come a long way.

Mohammad: Praise be Allah. I am the messenger of Allah on Earth.

Gabriel: Is Allah the same as God to the Jews and Christians?

Mohammad: The Jews and Christians are infidels. Allah is Allah.

Gabriel: Let's assume that God and Allah are the same. If all Men are worshiping the same God, what reason is there to call them infidels?

Mohammad: They are infidels because they will not convert to Moslem.

Gabriel: We could be going around and around for this question forever without getting any place. Tell us, how does one convert to Moslem?

Mohammad: Our followers are convinced that infidels should be converted by any means.

Gabriel: What if they refuse to convert?

Mohammad: Then they die by the sword.

Gabriel: That's pretty rough stuff.

Mohammad: That's the way of the world.

Gabriel: How was it that the Moslem religion spread so rapidly across the world from the shores of the Atlantic Ocean to the islands of the Pacific Ocean?

Mohammad: It was Allah's will. Of course it was an easy matter to follow the trade routes which were already centuries old. Forced conversion by rabid believers is very convincing.

Gabriel: From your history of the Moslem religion, there are several sects of Moslems who are frequently at one another's throats.

Mohammad: Yes, each sect is convinced that their interpretation of the Koran and other holy writings must be followed to the letter.

Gabriel: But why do they kill one another?

Mohammad: I have already told you. This is the way of the world.

Gabriel: Do you kill all infidels?

Mohammad: Oh, no. Our leaders have allowed infidels to live among us as long as they do not try to rule over us. Our caliphs in Spain and other countries lived well with the Jews. Together, they created what is known as The Golden Age of Spain. The philosophy, the poetry, the science and mathematics were unequaled.

Gabriel: So what happened to this happy state of affairs?

Mohammad: A rabid fundamentalist group from North Africa invaded Spain, violently disagreed with the Moslem religious practice in Spain, and that was that. Then, the Christians reconquered Spain and this Golden Age was gone.

Gabriel: And that was that?

Mohammad: I told you before. You can't beat human nature. Our followers are convinced they should destroy anything they feel is not strictly Moslem, and we don't want any infidels ruling over us.

Gabriel: Is this why you fought so many years against the Crusades?

Mohammad: The Crusades lasted for many years, and imposed severe hardships for my followers. As in all invasions they had some success, but in the end we were victorious. The best you can say for those Europeans was that they were barbarians. Even before they reached our shores, they pillaged and massacred the Jews in every country of Europe, especially Germany. We demand conversion. The Crusaders just murdered. That's the way of the world.

Gabriel: Why do you say they were barbarians?

Mohammad: We were a very sophisticated society. Philosophy, the Arts, our Literature, our Architecture are just a few of the areas that made us a highly cultured people.

Gabriel: If all you say is true, why do you kill the infidels who do not convert to Moslem and why do you kill each other?

Mohammad: I don't think you really understand. This is the way of the World.

Gabriel: No more questions. Thank you Mohammad. You have further convinced us that the men will never change.

Metatron: Mr. Snake, You may cross-examine Mohammad.

   Mr. Snake approaches Mohammad with his usual cocky demeanor.

Mr. Snake: Mohammad, do you know why you are here?

Mohammad: I suppose. This is Heaven isn't it? I came to Heaven riding on my horse from Jerusalem.

Mr. Snake: There is much more to it than that. You are in the Hall of Judgement. We are having a trial of Mankind to see whether he should continue to exist.

Mohammad: Oh.

Mr. Snake: From what I understand, your Koran and holy books include both the Torah and Christian teachings.

Mohammad: Yes, I had frequent association with Jews and am familiar with Christianity.

Mr. Snake: Did you make any changes in the Torah?

Mohammad: No, Abraham is our holy father and Ismail, our ancestor, as you know, was Abraham's first born.

Mr. Snake: But that is a deviation from the Torah which was given to the Israelites thousands of years before you.

Mohammad: The truth may take that much time to be revealed.

Mr. Snake: Do you say the same about Jacob and Esau?

Mohammad: Esau is our Arab branch of Abraham's family. He even married Ishmail's daughter.

Mr. Snake: Then you do have a close religious relationship with the Jews, so why do you refer to them as infidels?

Mohammad: As I have said before, all men must convert to Moslem or they are infidels. Our followers are correct feeling they will be blessed with 80 virgins in Heaven for being martyrs to Islam when they kill infidels.

Mr. Snake: Is this what you mean by rabid followers?

Mohammad: Now you are getting the right idea.

Mr. Snake: Your religion, what does it say about love and justice?

Mohammad: All Moslems must love Allah, and all Moslems must adhere to the laws of justice.

Mr. Snake: Tell us about the laws of justice.

Mohammad: The laws are clearly written in the holy books. They must be followed to the letter. Acts of crime such as stealing, adultery, usury are not tolerated. A man who steals has his arms chopped off no matter the reasons. Adultery is punished by stoning to death. Interest on loans must not be charged to other Moslems. Our religious leaders are the judges. Any leader of Moslem people is always right. No matter how he rules, he is always right. Let me repeat. Whoever is the leader is the absolute ruler. He must be followed without question. The sons of Islam are devoted to always following their leader no matter what he commands. We Arabs come from many different clans. There is strict adherence to the rules of the families within each clan. Heaven forbid, if one of them in a clan gets out of line or violates the rules of another clan.

Mr. Snake: Is there no compassion in your laws?

Mohammad: Our judges are not too compassionate. They follow the law to the letter.

Mr. Snake: One last question. Do you think that Mankind can tolerate the intolerance to infidels and the lack of love and compassion?

Mohammad: You live on Earth only to show your love for Allah. Infidels must convert to Moslem. My followers may use any means to convert them, or the infidels must die.

Mr. Snake shakes his head as he feels that he has not been able to challenge Mohammad in his case for Mankind.

Mr. Snake: No more questions.

Metetron: Angel Gabriel, do you have any other witnesses?

Gabriel: Yes, your honor. I wish to call Sol of Tarsus.

Sol is a balding thin man dresses in the mode of Roman citizens. His demeanor befits his confidence in his role on Earth.

Gabriel: Sol, I take it, that from your name, you were born in Tarsus. Is that correct?

Sol: Yes, that is true.

Gabriel: I understand that you are now known as Paul. Why did you change your name?

Sol: Well, to be honest, Sol sounds too Jewish.

Gabriel: Just what do you do?

Sol: I was sent to Damascus by the local Rabbis in Jerusalem to inspire Jews to return to Judaism. On the way, on my donkey, I had this inspiration to be a Christian. I found my calling. One might call me an Evangelist. I found it easy to find other men also to become Evangelists.

Gabriel: Were they also Jews?

Sol: No. I decided that Christianity had to break away from Judaism. All those rules and regulations such as circumcision and keeping Kosher were never to my liking. The rules and statutes had to be discarded. Man, were we successful! All we asked of new converts was to accept our Faith. Jesus would take care of everything else.

Gabriel: You knew Jesus?

Sol: Not really. When I was in Jerusalem, Jesus was already crucified. I did have problems with Peter and the other apostles. They were too Jewish for me.

Gabriel: Then I take it that nothing really changed in the lives of the convert to Christianity. Is that correct, or is there more to it than that?

Sol: How about calling me, Paul. I made some terrific changes to advance our new faith, Christianity. I decided that the story about Eve and the Snake described the Fall of Man. They really fell for that one. Then they could keep doing whatever they were doing. If you're bad you might as well enjoy it. From what I could see, I don't think many of these new converts from any of the pagan religions understood that when you really become a true Christian, you will give up sinning. Sinning seemed to be in their blood.

Gabriel: Paul, then what did that have to do with Christianity?

Paul: I convinced them that they could only be "saved" by accepting Christ.

Gabriel: You convinced them that every one of them had "fallen", or were disgraced?

Paul: Yep.

Gabriel: What other changes did you make?

Paul: I hit upon another great idea. I convinced them there was a New Covenant. They really like the New Covenant. The New Covenant were writings my letters to followers in the cities or other Christian writings of Apostles. We named all of these, "The Gospel". I don't think they really understood what we were trying to tell them but it made them feel good. We did this all over the Roman Empire. Most of them didn't know anything about the Old Covenant, so they fell for this one "hook, line and sinker".

Gabriel: What about the Jews who would not listen to you?

Paul: Who cares. The new Christians just picked up where the Romans left off. I think the Jews call this anti-Semitism. The Romans practiced anti-Semitism all over the Roman Empire, we made it almost world-wide. It seems that every Christian had a different reason for hating the

Jews-the Crucifixion, Economics, claiming that Jews were loyal to just being Jewish rather than being loyal to the country where they were born.

Economics was a very important reason, also. After picking their brains when these Christians didn't need them anymore, the Christians decided that only they should loan money to the royal houses and even the Popes. The Jewish money lenders charged only a small amount of interest for their loans. When the Christians took over the business of loaning money, the interest rates were so high, the royal families went back to the Jewish money lenders. The Christians didn't seem to get that one right.

Gabriel: So let me summarize your answers for a moment. Whatever Christians did with their lives or whatever their masters did to them, really meant little as long as they felt that they would end up in Heaven in Jesus' arms. And they could disregard the commandments in the "Old Testament" as they were of no importance in their lives. Hating Jews was just another reason for continuing the ancient ways of the world.

Paul: I think I did one hell'ov a job. I understand that Christianity has the largest body of adherents in the world.

Gabriel: I'm glad to hear you say that. Ever since then, they have been killing each other. Frequently killing anyone who was not a Catholic. So life on Earth goes on and on. No changes. The King of Moab and Machiaville would have been proud of you.

Gabriel: No more questions, the Prosecution rests.

Mr. Snake rises from his chair at the Defense table. He walks slowly in front of the witness stand carefully measuring his stride and his words.
Mr. Snake: Sol, I mean Paul, what is the most important thing between men?

Paul: We already know that the most important is love.

Mr. Snake: Just love.

Paul: Just love.

Mr. Snake: Was Love discovered by Christians?

Paul: The word, Love, is in any dictionary, but only we, Christians, really understand its importance.

Mr. Snake: In the Torah, it states, "You should love your God with all your might, with all your Soul". Is that part of your Love? Isn't this important?

Paul: Sure, that's important. But love between men is more important than any laws or customs.

Mr. Snake: You don't say. How about the Ten Commandments? Don't they also affect Mankind?

Paul: The Ten Commandments. It seems that everyone knows, and everyone pays them "lip service". Every day, men do not honor their Mothers and Fathers. Every day, men commit adultery. Every day, men commit murder. Every day, men covet another's possessions. Every day, men lie in court.

Mr. Snake: And love would stop men from committing all these sins?

Paul: If men loved Jesus enough, they would stop sinning.

Mr. Snake: Then all the commandments in the Torah are just so much drivel?

Paul: We respect the Old Testament, but now we have a New Testament. Christians have replaced Jews in God's eyes. It's hard for Jews to counter this.

Mr. Snake: There is a lot more in the Torah than the ritual of circumcision and keeping Kosher. The Jews were chosen to bring a new beginning to the world, and you have discarded it all?

Paul: Not really. We just gave them all a Christian "twist".

Mr. Snake: Do you mean you gave the entire Torah a Christian "twist"?

Paul: Certainly.

Mr. Snake: Let me get this straight. Men can continue doing whatever. Despots can continue doing what they've done for thousands of years as long as they accept Christianity. No one gives a damn about common man's life on Earth. It will be better or forgiven after they die. With all of your supposed Jewish upbringing, do you think that this is what God wanted of Humanity?

Paul: Why are you bringing up my Jewish upbringing? My letters, and those of others of my following, clearly state that I studied under the most auspicious Rabbis.

Mr. Snake: If that were true, nothing really rubbed off. It sounds to me that you had more Roman influences in your life than Jewish.

Paul: What's wrong with that?

Mr. Snake: Well for many many reasons but the most important is that we wouldn't be having this trial.

After a slight hesitation, Mr. Snake continues.

Mr. Snake: Among your holy books is the "Book of Revelations". Are you familiar with this book?

Paul: Yes, it is one of our holy books.

Mr. Snake: This book is filled with descriptions of Heaven, God and the Unrevealed. How do you account for this when the Jews don't even attempt to understand God and the Unrevealed other than the commandments in the Torah. They only use adjectives and adverbs to describe the Unrevealed in all of its aspects?

Paul: Jesus had risen from the dead. When they went to his sepulcher, it was empty. Then they saw him again living.

Mr. Snake: Were you there?

Paul: No, but all Christians have faith that Christ rose from the dead. It is the basis of our religion.

Mr. Snake: As I understand it, all of the Christian writings find their beginnings with only this supernatural event. That's a lot to build on when the Jews have only adjectives and adverbs. No more questions.

Metatron: Do you have any other witnesses to present to the court?

Gabriel: No, Your Honor.

Metatron: The trial will adjourn until tomorrow and we will have the summations by the Prosecution and the Defense.

All of the Souls who were present at the trial were gathering in the front of the Hall of Judgement.

Moses: There is one expression that has past on through all of the generations of our people. 'It looks bad for the Jews'. Now I think it looks bad for all Humanity.

Abraham: I'm not so sure. Mr. Snake presented some arguments that cannot be ignored no matter how bad Humanity has been. After listening to the witnesses at the trial, I really believe we were very wrong trying to convince everyone to understand and accept the true Spirituality because of our enlightenment. And that goes for all of us. Our wives really had a better handle on this than we.

Jacob: If only we had emphasized that Man inherited his bad instincts from the other animals. Perhaps then we could have successfully changed his animal instincts into accepting God's wishes for Man.

Moses: Perhaps your right, except for the unforgivable destruction that Man still continues on the environment. I can see Man finally accepting Isaiah's beating swords into plowshares, but his lack of stewardship of the Earth and the Seas is unforgivable.

Act Four

Act 4 Scene 1

It is the following morning. In the Piazza outside of the Hall of Judgement a curious parade is in progress. All four of the biblical Matriarchs, Eve, Zipporah, Abigail Adams, and Rabbi Akiba's wife are line dancing in two rows of four to the tune of YMCA. Eight other ladies rush over to join them. The music is loud and raucous.

"One, two, three, four!"
"Isms, Schisms, Ung a blyzim
We split hairs for piety
Showing our Faith's supremacy.
Vote in the Pope to be Vicar.
Immersed your bod in Jordan's river.
On your knees until they ache
Claim the cure from piety.
Allah's jihad, swing that sword
These will prove he is the Lord.
Isms, schisms, Ung a blysim."
One, two, three, four
Pick your Ism, just adore
Only a life knows the score.
One, two, three, four
Isms, schisms, Ung a blyzim."

Cherub 1: That's a first! I haven't seen that kind of dancing in Heaven before. The dancing and music are terrific. I bet everyone wants to join them.

Cherub 2: Look over there. The Cherubim and Seraphim of the jury are watching the ladies and swaying to the music. I wonder what they are thinking about all this?

Cherub 1: The ladies keep turning their heads and beaconing to the jury. You can bet those ladies are thinking for them.

Cherub 2: I can't think you will find any better Souls in Heaven than they. They really have the smarts, and know what messages will "sway" the jury.

Cherub 1: I would guess that they could be telling the jurors that they are the Mothers of Mankind. Men keep changing their darling little babies into men who are angry or hateful. After they grow up, all the troubles begin. I overheard Sarah talking with the other biblical Matriarchs. She was exasperated that most men are kind, charitable, and peace loving as individuals, but when you get them together into groups all hell breaks loose.

Cherub 2: Your right about that. Every nation and every religion is at fault. The nations of Europe use Christianity and Mohammedanism to justify their injustices. And the religious leaders always go along. Power and prestige are hard to say "no" to.

At the other side of the stage, the three Biblical Patriarchs, Noah and Moses are watching the line dancing.

Moses: What a parade! With the music and dancing, they look like they are leading King David into Jerusalem.

Abraham: Darn it, I should have taken dancing lessons so I could dance with Sarah. This must be the beginning of the Hora.

Noah: That's a joke. If this line dancing will become the Hora, then my wine drinking after the Flood will set off all the bacchanals. That wine is good stuff. It has been the center attraction for almost all festivals in every land of the world since the Flood.
Just as the line dancing is ending, Eve spies Mr. Snake.

Eve: Hey, Snake.

Mr. Snake: What do you want now?

Eve: I thought you were supposed to be defending Mankind.

Mr. Snake: You're starting all over again?

Eve: I was sitting with my girl friends in the back of the Hall yesterday. You looked pretty bad when you were cross-examining Mohammad. I know what happened when you out smarted me. How come you let Mohammad out smart you?

Mr. Snake: Look, what do you say when Mohammad had all the answers, no matter how he bent them from the truth.

Eve: Oh, so any kind of truth is also more than you can handle. I think you better be successful in the defense of Man or you will have me at your neck for eternity. Oh, I forgot. In the Garden of Eden, you didn't have a neck.

Mr. Snake turns quickly away from Eve and heads for the Hall of Judgement along with the Seraphim, Cherubim and the Souls.

Mr. Snake: (*talking to himself*) That broad is really driving me up the wall. I have to go into court to defend Mankind and she's just what I need now! What could I have been thinking of when I found her sitting under that apple tree.

The angel chorus ends the scene singing and dancing to a parody of "Don't sit under the apple tree."

Act 4 Scene 2

This scene returns to the Hall of Judgement. At the entrance of the hall are Souls carrying placards urging the jury to again pardon Mankind. Word from the We Finally Got It Right Gambler's Casino has the odds strongly in favor of the Prosecution 6 to 4. Every seat is filled with Cherubim, Seraphim, and Souls anxiously awaiting the summations by the Prosecution and the Defense. Noah, Abraham and Moses are seated together.

Moses: If we had only realized what God really wanted from us was to make Man aware of his uncontrollable instincts that he inherited from animals. Instead we made ourselves paragons of virtue. What a mistake!

Abraham: We must not lose hope. If God has made Mankind the Crown of Creation, assuredly He will pardon Man's iniquities.

Noah: Fat chance. He knocked off Mankind at the Flood and, from what I can see, he will do it again. The destruction of Sodom and Gomorrah, and the penalty that Moses talked God out of for worshiping the Golden Calf, were nothing compared to the Flood. I'm sure this time, man's time has run out.

The judge, Metatron, enters the hall and takes his seat high above the assembly.

Bailiff: Hear Ye, Hear Ye, His Honor, Metatron. Order in the court!

Metatron: (*Striking his gavel several times. Absolute quiet descends from the assembly*) We will now hear the summations of the Prosecution and then the Defense. This has been a lengthy trial but one that is of universal importance. The prosecution will now present its final arguments followed by the Defense. Then the jury will retire and consider its verdict. The final verdict will require 75 percent of the votes, or nine votes in favor from the twelve jurors.

The Angel Gabriel rises from his chair at the Prosecutor's table and walks carefully to face the jury. In his hand is a small index card with notes listing the comments he might wish to present.

Gabriel: Members of the jury, my remarks will show that Man has failed to change his ways throughout all of history. This may be blasphemy, but, at Creation, I don't think God had very good material to start with in creating Man. Throughout the biblical years, throughout the rise and fall of vast empires, to the massive destruction of the present times on Earth, Man continues to reveal his true character. There is only one word that can describe his character-Man is deadly. He will kill or destroy without reason or provocation. Whatever qualities of man that enlightened people tried to change for the better is ignored or is belittled by the vast majority of mankind. I agree that to "Err is Human", but there is a point where man's errors go beyond any notion of forgiveness. Man has past any point where he can be forgiven. I have presented four witnesses for the Prosecution, the King of Moab, Machiavelli, Mohammad, and Paul the Apostle. Many men could have been equally as good witnesses for the Prosecution. Instead of the King of Moab, the Emperors of Rome, or Hitler, or Stalin, or many others could be as qualified. Each of them proclaimed that the

World of men will never change. Machiavelli studied and wrote books on how to govern in the face of the fact that men will never change. Christianity is used by all European nations to claim racial or religious superiority. "Render to Caesar", in reality, has no meaning when the Papacy renders edicts to the countries that have little to do with religious guidance. Mohammad founded a worldwide religion knowing that man will not change. His followers unleashed a Xenophobia that continues to rock the entire World. All non-Moslems are infidels. Sol or Paul established a religion that focused on salvation-whatever that means. For both Christianity and Islam, life on Earth is relatively meaningless. Many of the religions of the Eastern world still worship idols or men. These religions often desire peace between men, or mental peace for individuals, but they have little understanding of God. Man cannot use his imagination to gain understanding of the Unrevealed, nor can he be a part of the Unrevealed.

Gabriel notices that his attack on Man is creating restlessness in the jury box.

Gabriel: Let me briefly add that Mankind has little appreciation for the importance of animals in their natural state. He has disrupted the natural food chains, and polluted the land, seas and the air unconscious of the harm he has done. But I have said enough. Let the jury study the facts. They cannot be deigned.

Metatron: We will take a short recess before proceeding with the summation by the Defense.

The three Patriarchs, Moses and Noah meet in the hall outside the assembly.

Noah: Well, gentlemen, if you think the world was destroyed by the Flood because of violence and immorality, Mankind does not have a chance now. All Man's evils have multiplied many times in the course of History. Man is hopeless and thus he is helpless.

Moses: I think that all we can do is to go back into the synagogue and pray to God for forgiveness for Mankind.

With their heads lowered in resignation with tears streaming from their eyes, they head for the synagogue.

Act 4 Scene 3

The scene reopens in the hall of Assembly. The three Patriarchs, Moses and Noah have returned from the synagogue with ashes on their foreheads. They continue to wipe the tears from their eyes with their sleeves.

Metatron: Mr. Snake, you may now speak for the Defense.

Mr. Snake removes his rattlesnake jacket, rolls up his sleeves, approaches the jury box with a self-assurance that penetrates the minds of the jurors.

Mr. Snake: We have heard the summation by the learned Prosecutor and I must admit everything he has said and every witness he has presented is evidence that Mankind should not continue to exist. However, we must look at the problems from an entirely different direction. There is much more to be considered than the brutality of the Kings of Moab, the Hitlers, the Stalins and all the other maniacs who governed countries. There is much more to be considered than Man's neglect of the land, the seas, the skies, and all the plants and animals therein. And we can throw in the horrible devastations imposed on the other men and women by religious zealots as well.

The angel Gabriel leans back in his chair at the Prosecution table with a beaming smile. He appears convinced that Mr. Snake has conceded and the case is his.

Mankind is a "work in progress". There is a field of discovery that digs up fossils of Man from different areas of the world trying to determine the earliest evidence of Human inhabitation. It's been a tough dig, but they have discovered fossilized "human" bones dating millions of Earth years ago. A scientist, named Willford Libby, devised dating these bones by a Carbon 14 technique. These fossils are found all over the world, in China, in Africa by Richard Leakey, and many other anthropologists. These fossilized bones are thought to be hundreds of thousands of years old. Later in the chronology of Man, the Neanderthal Man, and later the CroMagnum Man, living 35,000 to 10,000 years ago, were discovered. They were judged to be closely related to Modern man. In their current analysis, these scientists are trying to confirm that Man is an offshoot of the family of Apes. For the sake of argument, let us assume that they are correct.

Now the Angel Gabriel is less certain of his victory. He is listening intently as Mr. Snake proceeds.

There are numerous similar physical characteristics of Man to Apes. From Professor Freud's study of human behavior, he has testified that Man has inherited instincts and drives from wild or undomesticated animals. All undomesticated or wild animals are integral parts of the natural food chain. All undomesticated animals will eat or be eaten. Let us examine just a few of the similarities of the behavior of Mankind of those of wild or undomesticated animals noting Professor Freud's testimony.

Loud murmuring can be heard from the back of the hall.

Bailiff: We must have order in the court.

Metatron: As I have said many times before, you Souls must remain quiet or I will clear the court again!

Mr. Snake: Once Man discovered that he was naked, he was no longer a part of the natural food chain, but he still retained animal instincts and animal drives. In its place, he tilled and soil, domesticated animals, gained free will and an unrestrained imagination. Where undomesticated animals will fight to the death to preserve their territorial integrity for the preservation of the best physical traits of their progeny, Man fights to the death to prevent invasion of his territorial borders. With unswerving allegiance, he will demonstrate his animal aggressiveness by conquering or killing other men. He even maintains that his countrymen are superior to other people and this gives him the right to destroy them. In the natural food chain, the undomesticated animal kills for food, but, at all other times, the "Lion lies down with the Lamb. Man kills for sport. God has commanded Man, "Do not disturb the Natural food chain of land and sea animals that cleanse the world". Man has ignored this warning. But, I repeat, Man is still a work in progress.
Each time Mr. Snake repeats the sentence, "Man is a work in progress" the jury seems more and more impressed.

With the creation of Adam and Eve, the "animal man" recognizes that he is more than just an animal. Man is beginning to recognize true Spirituality. This devotion to true Spirituality has nothing to do with man's senses, his imagination, what he observes, or his domination of other men. This work in progress continues with Noah who was righteous among all other man of his time. Noah recognized that the invisible living God created all by His will. This work in progress continues with Abraham and Sarah and their descendants. This little family, and those men and women who converted, understood that these debasing inherited drives and instincts of Man must be suppressed. New instincts must be those of peace, charity, tolerance and understanding between all men. This must be the way of living for all time on Earth. All promises of salvation are only pagan zealousness. But, as yet, this work in progress has had little acceptance.

There have been worldwide Monotheistic religions whose tenets profess peace, charity, tolerance and understanding, but all are perverted. True Spirituality is lost when charismatic "Messiahs" or overzealous men and women convince their followers that salvation will follow if one would only believe. And so members of the jury, understand that Man has the foundation and understanding to progress, if he is given another chance to exist. Man's knowledge of God and His wishes for Mankind have been only a few years in the making. It has only been a few years, and there have been men and women who recognize that Man must suppress his animal instincts. God willing, man will become the man God wishes him to be. Given the chance, man can and will do this.

Before I complete my summation, let me remind the jury that this small band of men, women and their converts have become psychological mutations from the rest of Mankind. They maintain their convictions in spite of all desires to exterminate them.

This Work in Progress has progressed into a nation with the sons and daughters of peoples who were rejected by other nations. America is far different from all other nations past or present. The citizens of this country, along with the children of this small band and their converts, live side by side in almost complete friendship and tolerance. The inventiveness, ingenuity, and hard work of its citizens is truly miraculous. Assassinations for political gain is almost unknown. Leadership is

by selection from all citizens who wish to vote. All other countries suffer by intense privation from hate and intolerance from within or from their neighboring countries. Although they have been in many wars, this nation has solved the disgrace of slavery, and has built a nation so prosperous that every citizen has reached a standard of living unparalleled in the history of the world. After each of the major world wars, America has rebuilt the countries of their enemies. If the promise to Abraham was "A Land of Milk and Honey, here, too, America is a land of milk and honey. In the last analysis, they have almost fulfilled God's desire for Mankind.

After Mr. Snake had completed his summation, uncontrollable shouting by the Souls filled the hall. The judge, Angel Metatron, has lost his stern demeanor and allows the shouting to continue.

Metatron: The Defense and the Prosecution have presented their case. The jury will now retire, and consider its verdict. You members of the jury have a heavy responsibility. This trial was ordered by God. The fate of Mankind may be in your hands.

Act 4 Scene 4

The Finale

The scene opens to the far left of the stage at the entrance to the We Finally Got It Right Reformed Gamblers Casino. The betting board is now almost even money. Betters who lost at the end of each day were tearing up their "chits". Two of the Biblical Matriarchs are walking past the casino.

Rachel: If I find out that my husband has been betting on this trial, he better not come home.

Rebecca: Loosen up, Rachel, we all have a little larceny in our souls. Remember when you were on that camel on your way to Canaan with Jacob and Leah. You talked your Dad, Laban, out of searching under your saddle blanket.

Rachel: That was different.

Rebecca: Come off of it. We've used this trick on our fathers and husbands forever.
Rachel: OK, but he better be home for dinner by six.

Rebecca: I'm sure he will. The trial should be over in the afternoon.

Rachel and Rebecca are walking near the Hall of Judgement when they see their husbands standing with Abraham, Moses, and Noah. Sarah, and Ziporrah are standing with them.

Rebecca: There they are. All of the other Souls are standing together with them. We better go over to see what's going on.

Rachel: Jacob, What's going on?

Jacob: Everyone is going bonkers trying to guess what the outcome of the trial will be. I think Moses is still optimistic that God will give Mankind another chance. Noah is convinced that Mankind is all washed up.

Off to the side Eve is walking slowly with Mr. Snake.

Eve: Snake, come and sit on this bench with me.

Mr. Snake: Not again! Look, Eve, I've tried my best for mankind even though men and women have not thought well of me on Earth. What more can you bitch about? We haven't been on the best of terms here in Heaven.
Eve: I promise you. No more finger pointing. Since your summation, I have a different impression about you. We women can't completely forgive you about the pain at childbirth, but women do have to put up with a lot during our lives. Maybe we are pushing the pain at childbirth a little too strong. After delivery, when our husbands see the miracle of their newborn baby, it gives us a leg

up on our husbands. His new baby is his joy and wonderment. Then we can turn on the charm and he's breakfast, lunch and dinner.

Lately, I've been wondering about our time in the Garden of Eden. After I ate the apple from the Tree of Knowledge, Adam and I were sent out of the Garden into the world to make our way as best we could. God allowed you to stay in the Garden although he punished you by making you crawl on your belly. Even though we were both penalized, we were both admitted to Heaven. From your defense of Mankind at this trial, God must have allowed you into Heaven for this very purpose. Why don't we walk over to where the Patriarchs and their wives are congregated.

Mr. Snake: I'm not so sure they will welcome me.

Eve: Are you kidding? You are about all they have in hopes of saving Mankind.

The scene shifts to the synagogue. On one wall of the synagogue is an enormous Torah that symbolizes the diminutive importance of Man. Noah, the Patriarchs, and Moses are discussing the future of Mankind.

Noah: Now that the trial is over and we are awaiting God's decision, I must admit that Mr. Snake's defense of Mankind may be the winning argument. Man must have more time to overcome his bestial instincts.

Abraham: But let us consider that we have all failed during our lives to influence Men. We and all of the men who followed by leading exemplary lives really meant nothing in the stream of human history.

Jacob: The Torah tells us many things. God fully knows the uncontrollable imaginations of men. The few lines relating the murder of Abel by Cain reveals to us the emotional differences between men. There are no two men alike.

Moses: Yes, this is the purpose giving Man the Torah. There must be well defined boundaries to Man's behavior that cannot be altered by Man's reasoning.

Abraham: "To be fruitful and multiply" does not give Man the permission to destroy the Balance of Nature . He is to preserve the Balance of Nature, not destroy it. Senseless killing of other animals and overpopulation leads only to starvation. The "Lion will lay down with the Lamb" as long as he is not hungary. This is not the message of peace between men. It is the law of nature.

Noah: Man must understand Mr. Snakes argument that his inherited animal drives cannot be clothed in religious garb. National or religious superiority is an anathema to Man's existence. Anti-Semitism clouds all reasoning. The question of "Where is God" is not a condemnation of God because of Man's Inhumanity to Man. Man must control his predatory animal instincts.

Abraham: Man is the Crown of Creation. He must know that he cannot act like other animals. Purposeless territorial wars have been the definition of history. That the German people are superior

to other people and nations gives Mankind tyrants and maniacs like Hitler. There must be rule by just laws, not the whim of dictators. Welcome the stranger is my contribution to Mankind.

Moses: Let us leave the synagogue and join our wives. God's decision on the future of Mankind will soon be known in Heaven.

The scene shifts to the Hall of Judgement. Every seat is filled anxiously awaiting the jury's decision.

Bailiff: Order in the court!
Metatron: Members of the jury, have you reached a verdict?

Spokesman: Your Honor, we have been arguing for hours trying to reach a verdict. At times we almost reached nine votes for the Prosecution, but then one juror would change his vote. I'm afraid we are a hung jury.

Metatron: I, too, have listened carefully to both the witnesses for the Defense and for the Prosecution. Angel Gabriel and Mr. Snake have been most elegant in their presentations to the court. I feel confident that God's judgment will soon be known.

Mr. Snake is thanked by all the Patriarchs and Matriarchs. He is the center of attention.

Moses: We do not know what the out come of this trial will be. Your efforts to save Mankind were exactly on the spot. Much more relevant than we were able to do during our lifetimes. Believing we were Paragons of Virtue is impossible to sell to the rest of the World. It is so clear now that we misunderstood God's messages.

Mr. Snake is in the center of a large semicircle in front of a bush. Suddenly a large fire is burning at the corner of the stage without consuming the bush. Thunderous music from Beethoven's symphony accentuates each line. Each line repeated twice like an echo.

"Peoples of the world"
"Your future is to be granted one more time."
"I am a jealous God."
"Let not your imaginations wander into the Heaven."
"You are not animals"
"You are my Crown of the Universe."
"Your lives are only on Earth."
"Do Not Hope to Know the Unrevealed"
"Follow my Commandments"
"Nothing else matters."

About The Author

Dr Steinberg has authored two books and many medical articles related to his research and clinical studies.

"Expanding Your Horizons" is a motivational book for young adults.

"Cataclysm" is a science novel based on the past events best explained by the abnormal wobble of the axis of rotation of the Earth. Like "Candide", Cataclysm is also a critique of the dogma of modern scientific theory.

Printed in the United States
by Baker & Taylor Publisher Services